COUNTERINSURGENCY

COUNTERINSURGENCY

Theory and Reality

DANIEL WHITTINGHAM AND STUART MITCHELL

CASEMATE

Oxford & Philadelphia

Published in Great Britain and the United States of America in 2021 by
CASEMATE PUBLISHERS
The Old Music Hall, 106–108 Cowley Road, Oxford OX4 1JE, UK
and
1950 Lawrence Road, Havertown, PA 19083, USA

Hardcover Edition: ISBN 978-1-61200-948-3
Digital Edition: ISBN 978-1-61200-949-0

A CIP record for this book is available from the British Library

Printed and bound in in the United Kingdom by TJ Books

Typeset by Versatile PreMedia Services (P) Ltd.

For a complete list of Casemate titles, please contact:

CASEMATE PUBLISHERS (UK)
Telephone (01865) 241249
Email: casemate-uk@casematepublishers.co.uk
www.casematepublishers.co.uk

CASEMATE PUBLISHERS (US)
Telephone (610) 853-9131
Fax (610) 853-9146
Email: casemate@casematepublishers.com
www.casematepublishers.com

Front cover: A Georgian soldier provides security during a patrol outside of the Qaleh
Musa Pain village in Helmand province, Afghanistan, March 12, 2015. (U.S.
Dept of Defense)

Dedicated to our families.

Contents

Acknowledgements		ix
Introduction		xi
Timeline		xxvii
1	The Roots of Counterinsurgency	1
2	Counterinsurgency, 1945–2000	35
3	A British Way in Counterinsurgency? 1945–2000	61
4	Modern Counterinsurgency: Iraq and Afghanistan 2001–14	97
Conclusion		147
Select Bibliography		153
Index		161

Acknowledgements

Writing this work would have been impossible without the support of the Department of History at the University of Birmingham and the War Studies Department at the Royal Military Academy Sandhurst. Both of us benefited from lengthy periods of study leave, which provided the time and space to conduct research and pen the book. In particular, Dan would like to thank successive heads of school Corey Ross and Sabine Lee, and heads of department Nick Crowson, Elaine Fulton, and Matt Houlbrook for their support. Stuart would like to thank his departmental colleagues for their wisdom and camaraderie and specifically thank Duncan Anderson, Chris Mann, James Kitchen and Klaus Schmider who provided valuable advice at key moments. We both owe a tremendous debt of gratitude to the staff of the libraries and archives that have supported this book. Specific mention must be made to Andrew Orgill and John Pearce of the RMAS library whose knowledge and tireless work provided immeasurable assistance to us, and the ever-helpful staff at The National Archives and British Library.

We both realise that we are fortunate to have some incredible academic colleagues and mentors who have offered their insights and encouragement throughout this project. We would like to thank Gary Sheffield, John Bourne, Stephen Badsey, Spencer Jones, Aimée Fox, Matthew Ford, Alan James, William Philpott, Jonathan Boff, Jonathan Krause, Paul Ramsey, and Christopher Duffy. We would also like to offer our thanks to Ruth Sheppard, Isobel Fulton, Alison

Boyd and the staff of Casemate Publishing who have been diligent and patient with us during the complicated publication process.

Our friends and families have been amazing. Stuart would particularly like to thank Chris McDowall, Sarah Acton, Andrew Slater, Kelly and Dan McNicholas, Abigail Thomas and Snowy for providing a Manchester sanctuary away from writing. We would both like to show our appreciation to Fotoula Hatzantonis, who has been a source of enduring strength and always there to offer kind words of encouragement. Stuart would like to acknowledge Abe, his little black cat, who was often perched on his shoulder while writing, and most importantly his mother, Amanda Taylor, whose patience and understanding made this book possible. Dan would like to thank his family for their constant support. Dan wrote most of the drafts of his portions of the book while away in Turkey: he would like to thank Orhan amca, Canan teyze, Ayşe teyze, and Ece for their hospitality during his stay. Most of all, he would like to thank his wife Gönenç for her love and support.

Introduction

'Mission Accomplished'

BANNER ON THE USS *ABRAHAM LINCOLN*, 1 MAY 2003

On 1 May 2003 US President George W. Bush touched down on the aircraft carrier USS *Abraham Lincoln*. In a carefully choreographed arrival, he shook hands and had photos taken with the crew and commander of the US Navy vessel, while wearing a military flight suit. He had not flown the S-3B Viking jet which arrived on the carrier but that mattered little. The message was clear: Bush was a President who got things done. Later that same day, now in a more traditional black suit, the President stood in front of the assembled navy crew and world media with a 'mission accomplished' banner adorning the conning tower behind him. His speech left a clear sense that the war in Iraq was over. 'Major combat operations in Iraq have ended. In the battle of Iraq, the United States and her Allies have prevailed.' Clapping and cheers erupted from the crowd of serving sailors. The message resonated; the longest deployment since Vietnam – ten months – was nearly finished. The camera promptly cut to the banner. The hard work had been done.

As Bush's speech continued, he emphasised the precision, speed and boldness of the American forces' attack. They had destroyed enemy divisions from a great distance, while Marines and soldiers sped across 350 miles of hostile ground. Despite paying lip service

George W. Bush on the deck of USS *Abraham Lincoln*.

to the security and reconstruction task they now faced, the President had described Operation *Iraqi Freedom* in traditional, conventional terms. But the war was not over and it had already begun to change. Mass gatherings took place in Fallujah on 28 and 30 April 2003, leading to indiscriminate shooting by the US airborne troops stationed in the city. Thirteen civilians were killed and 91 injured. More widely, rioting and looting began breaking out. Iraq was fracturing along sectarian lines and radical elements began to move in to exploit the lawlessness. In response, most senior American political and military leaders attempted to wage conventional war on an unconventional opponent. They failed to understand the changing environment. They failed to understand that they were now facing a nascent insurgency.

Understanding the characteristics of the war being fought is integral for any commander or politician. Insurgencies can evolve in parallel to conventional operations, using a variety of tactics and methods. Their clandestine nature can obscure the danger posed to existing civil, military or social structures. Civil disorder can bleed into rioting, which might end up leading to more organised resistance. Militaries and politicians alike have frequently struggled to switch from a mindset of conventional operations to stabilisation and development. In 2003, President Bush's triumphalism made him a hostage to fortune. Iraq was already a fertile ground for an insurgency. It was a decision he came to regret in 2008 when he admitted in an interview with CNN that: 'It conveyed the wrong message.' But the failure ran deeper than a banner and hubris. Iraq was the latest failure of a stronger conventional force to recognise that the war they were fighting had changed.

Insurgencies and counterinsurgencies have been the most common form of warfare throughout the 20th century. Since 1900, the United Kingdom has been almost continually engaged in a succession of small wars. Before 2016, only 1968 was a bloodless year for the armed forces. Yet despite this, these wars have remained largely overshadowed by their more conventional and intensive counterparts. This is understandable: major state-on-state conflicts, such as the World Wars, have led to enormous casualties in absolute terms and in a relatively short period of time. Conventional operations, which see regular forces of one or more states fight another, often have a marked effect on both the militaries and societies of those involved. Counterinsurgencies, on the other hand, can be much more diverse in their impact. They are frequently influenced by regional conditions or the actions of specific leaders, and they have often had ambiguous outcomes. Going further, historians and soldiers alike have struggled to pin down what defines a counterinsurgency campaign. The combatting of an insurgency is so intimately wrapped up with criminality, political violence and terrorism that it has been difficult for experts to agree where one label ends and another begins. This book is our attempt to shed light on this difficult topic and to explore how the theories that have shaped counterinsurgency have frequently smoothed over the difficult realities of these campaigns.

This is a multi-national history of small wars, intended to be an introduction to a complex topic. While many academics have sought to critique existing and historical methods of counterinsurgency, few have been able to explain a better way. Our intention is not to judge but to provide an overview of the field of study and examples of how counterinsurgent practices have evolved since the late 19th century. In doing so, both the student of war and the military practitioner (often one and the same) might better understand the complexities of insurgencies and counterinsurgencies. We hope it might prompt the reader into asking further questions.

Definitions

The first difficulty faced when dealing with counterinsurgency is the definition. It is framed by its oppositional relationship to insurgency. It is a relative term, requiring some understanding of the context. This is not unusual in military matters. Other terms suffer similar problems: conventional or irregular warfare, symmetrical and asymmetrical, high or low intensity, small wars or major ones; all convey a sense of the type of war but generally seen through one dominant perspective, usually a NATO one. If this was not tricky enough to navigate, campaigns often described as insurgencies frequently feature acts of terrorism against civilians, significant criminality or combat between conventionally organised forces. Civil wars add a further layer of terminological confusion. To unravel this maze of terms, it is worth starting by recognising that what constitutes counterinsurgency is dependent upon how insurgencies are defined. This has unsurprisingly varied but there are some broad definitions.

Some scholars have defined insurgency as a method employed when a disparity in power exists between the two sides. Steven Metz tried to break from what he described as the 'orthodox conceptualization' of counterinsurgency and offered a simplified definition with a greater emphasis on non-Western or patronage-based political structures. This linked his definition of what an insurgency is to the methods an insurgent group uses to achieve its objectives. 'One way to avoid common (and largely useless) debates over whether a particular organization or a particular conflict is or is not an insurgency… is to think of it as a *type of strategy* that can be used in many types of conflicts by many types of organizations' (Metz, 'Rethinking Insurgency', in Rich and Duyvesteyn (eds.), *The Routledge Handbook of Insurgency and Counterinsurgency*, p.37). This idea was based upon the work of Isabelle Duyvesteyn and Mario Fumerton who explored the differences between terrorism and insurgency. They concluded that terrorism might function as a tactic within a broad insurgent strategy and might be usefully employed to coerce a participant or particular social group into a certain course of action – or conversely to deter them from one. There is much to commend in this approach. It fits neatly with what some insurgent theorists saw as guerrilla warfare. Carlos Marighella opened his *Minimanual of the Urban Guerrilla* (1969) with the following definition: 'The urban guerrilla is a person who fights the military dictatorship with weapons, using unconventional methods' (p.9). This conception of insurgency emphasises the importance of the weaker side developing its resources. That might be through the recruitment of fighters, alliance building, economic development, training or acquiring new weaponry. Metz places insurgencies along a spectrum with informal groups using cells or loose networks at one end. These smaller groups' aim is to build capacity. Larger organisations with more formal hierarchies sit at the other end of the spectrum. These groups might have grander objectives, for example attempting to supplant the existing social or political structures in a nation, region or even globally. Insurgencies may move along this spectrum, changing in structure, objective and focus as they develop or are challenged.

Strategy is generally accepted as the coordination and direction of national or organisational resources to achieve a war's political objectives. This has given rise to the idea of the three levels of war. Strategy sits at the top, operations beneath that and tactics at the bottom. If strategy is how to win wars, then the tactical level is how to achieve specific military objectives or, to put it more crudely, winning battles. Operations is the most difficult to define and concerns the sequencing of battles to achieve a significant or decisive strategic outcome. Strategy, then, sits at the intersection between military action and politics.

Defining insurgency as a strategy has drawbacks. Strategy is no less of a loaded term than insurgency. Despite Metz recognising and accounting for the importance of politics, critics like Gian Gentile have observed that defining insurgency in such a way has led to counterinsurgent approaches creating a 'strategy of tactics' (Gentile, 'Strategy of Tactics', p.5–17). In other words, it focuses on ideas that might help to fight battles, not how to win wars.

This friction is complicated by the use of insurgent strategies by the stronger side. States have proven themselves willing to adopt the methods of the insurgent. In April 2014, Russia inserted clandestine military forces into eastern Ukraine to aid and organise separatist elements. They were not the first. The Allied powers coordinated partisan, resistance activity against the Axis during World War II, while T. E. Lawrence's support for the Arab Revolt during World War I served as an adjunct to conventional operations in Egypt and Palestine. In that same war, Paul von Lettow-Vorbeck, the commander defending German East Africa (roughly covering modern-day Tanzania), frequently used hit and run tactics, ambushes and supply raids to undermine British efforts to conquer the colony. These sorts of insurgent approaches were not limited to supplementing conventional strategies during the World Wars. The Jewish revolt by the Stern Gang and Irgun in Palestine (1945–48) prompted the British to employ similar tactics to those of the Jewish insurgents. This was not an isolated occurrence for Britain as it attempted to manage its withdrawal from empire. During the Aden Emergency (1963–67), the British SAS disguised themselves as Arabs and employed 'keeni-meeni' tactics. These involved luring Arab nationalist rebels of the National Liberation Front (NLF) or Front for the Liberation of South Yemen (FLOSY) into close-quarters ambushes, where they could be killed or captured. The frequent adoption of insurgent tactics by counterinsurgent forces shows that regular troops are more than capable of acting irregularly. The attempts by states to beat insurgents at their own game, or to support conventional approaches, have blurred the lines to the extent that modern British counterinsurgency doctrine talks of 'hybrid threats' and 'adversaries' (*Army Field Manual*, p.1). State-sponsored special forces allied to insurgent groups do not fit the popular perception of militarily weaker revolutionaries. The goals and structures of an insurgent organisation matter. Thus, the political objective that the strategy is directed towards must play some part in defining the nature of an insurgency.

More traditional definitions of insurgency, and counterinsurgency, have positioned it as a form of war. The British Army's Field Manual *Countering Insurgency* (2010) makes this explicit on the first page of the first chapter: 'Counterinsurgency is warfare; it is distinctly political, not primarily military; and it involves the people, the government and the military. The strength of the relationship between these three groups generally determines the outcome of the campaign.' The US Army and Marine Corps *Army Field Manual 3-24: Counterinsurgency* (FM 3-24) was published in 2009 and argues along the same line: 'Insurgency and counterinsurgency (COIN) are complex subsets of warfare' (*Army Field Manual 3-24*, p.12). Australian doctrine in *Land Warfare Doctrine LWD 3-0-1 Counterinsurgency* also follows a similar line of reasoning:

'COIN represents a part of the spectrum of conflict that requires the Australian Army's attention both now and into the foreseeable future' (Chap.1-1). So, what is war? One military theorist stands above the others in establishing the most widely accepted definition: the Prussian military thinker, Carl von Clausewitz (1780–1831).

Clausewitz, a soldier scholar who had experienced the Napoleonic Wars first-hand, penned perhaps the most influential work of military theory ever written, *On War*. In this, he defined war as: 'an act of violence to compel our opponent to do our will' (p.7). This has come to form the outline for modern military definitions of war and so too insurgency and counterinsurgency. The Clausewitzian definition of war is contingent upon three core factors: violence, politics and organisation. War requires physical violence; without it, the dispute remains political. One of Britain's principal counterinsurgency theorists, Frank Kitson in *Bunch of Five* (1977), understood this when he wrote: 'Unfortunately there is no such thing as insurgency without violence because without it, opposition would not amount to insurgency' (p.xiii). There is a growing ambiguity in the word violence, but here, Clausewitz could not be clearer – violence is physical force. In the complex world of modern geopolitics, various pressures may be applied – such as economic sanctions, diplomatic isolation or cyber-crime – to achieve policy goals, but those alone do not equate to war. They may ultimately be interpreted as a cause for war or an act of aggression but, until physical force is applied, they cannot constitute war if Clausewitz's definitions are used. Perhaps, now more than ever before, there is a pressure with so-called 'hybrid threats' to move away from this definition, but no one has offered a more useful one for modern militaries.

Violence does not occur in a vacuum; it arises from political direction. When Clausewitz wrote of doing or fulfilling 'our will', he was referring to the political aims to be achieved. The emphasis on political will does more than set the ends to be achieved in war; it organises the application of violence. Rioting may happen as a result of a political grievance and have some loosely defined objective, but it lacks the formal organisation that would define it as war. But groups brought together in the wake of riots who then take more considered action to equip themselves and to use violence to achieve their common will fit the Clausewitzian definition. It, therefore, frames the definition of insurgency. This very scenario occurred in the wake of violent protests in Syria against the Ba'athist regime of Bashar Al-Assad on 15 March 2011. The heavy-handed response by Syrian government forces against civilians led to defections by some officers and soldiers, who went on to form the Free Syrian Army on 29 July 2011. With two competing authorities, both willing to use violence to achieve their aims, rioting and protests had become an insurgency. Syria descended into civil war.

One further Clausewitzian concept is worth explanation because it has influenced how armies have conceptualised both war and insurgency. The 'wondrous trinity' (sometimes translated as 'paradoxical trinity') was Clausewitz's attempt to identify the elements of the unchanging nature of war. These elements were violence, formed by hatred, and enmity, created as a result of 'blind natural instinct' (often summarised simply as passion); the interplay of probabilities and chance that make it the 'free activity of the soul' – that is to say the creativity of man taming the wilder turns of fortune; and finally reason, which subordinates it to a 'political instrument'. Violence, chance and reason form the primary trinity, but confusion has abounded owing to Clausewitz's next paragraph, which explains that each of these factors relates predominantly, but not always exclusively, to elements of the state – people, military and government. Violence or passion 'concerns more the people', probability and chance 'concerns more the general and his army' (more broadly the military) and reason 'more the government'. Clausewitz qualifies the latter by observing that: 'the political objects are the concern of the government alone' (p.20). Some scholars, like John Keegan, Martin van Creveld and Mary Kaldor, have placed this state-centred secondary trinity ahead of that of the first. They are in good company. As Hew Strachan has shown in *The Direction of War*, Colin Powell – former US Secretary of State – had made a similar mistake in his reflections upon Vietnam.

So too did Colonel Harry Summers in his highly influential account of the US failure in that conflict, *On Strategy* (1981). As Strachan notes: 'what for Clausewitz was the primordial trinity became the secondary one: his interpretation had been reversed to put the components of the state in front of the attributes which make up war' (Strachan, *Direction of War*, p.50). This has led to many of his insights on non-inter-state war such as insurgency and counterinsurgency being discounted as irrelevant. The relationship of the three primary factors – violence, chance and reason – is not static and their interaction defines the character of any war.

By defining insurgency and counterinsurgency as a form of warfare, NATO definitions have drawn heavily on Clausewitz's definition of war itself. The notion of organised violence to achieve a political objective is a common theme, while the differentiation between the trinities provides some indication of where militaries have sought to find their definitions. The previously quoted British description of 'counterinsurgency as warfare' added that it: 'involves the people, the government and the military' (*Army Field Manual*, p.1). The same doctrinal manual defines insurgency as an 'organised, violent subversion used to effect or prevent political control, as a challenge to established authority' (Ibid, p.1–4).' The artefacts of Clausewitz should be clear, but the greater specifics of the goal separate this definition of insurgency from the broader definition of war. The manual continues by providing some examples of motivation for insurgency, such as ideology, religion, ethnicity or class, as well as observing the variety of aims which might encompass territorial control, restitution of a grievance or the overthrow of government. Perhaps most critically, the manual also states: 'While the majority of insurgencies will have a strategy some may not' (Ibid, p.1–4). The divisions within insurgencies over the goals to be achieved and the methods employed to do so may undermine an insurgent organisation's capacity to implement a coordinated strategy. The lure of criminality can ultimately become an aim unto itself. The Revolutionary Armed Forces of Colombia (FARC) faced these problems as it drifted away from its Marxist-Leninist, Maoist roots towards 'Bolívarian populism' that, as Thomas Marks has contended, 'had little appeal in Colombia' (Marks, 'Regaining the Initiative', in Marston and Malkasian (eds), *Counterinsurgency in Modern Warfare*, p.211). This pulled the organisation toward violent action rather than slower mobilisation of the people and a wide support base. To fund this, the cultivation of narcotics, drug trafficking, as well as kidnapping and ransom, became the primary means of sustaining the insurgency until the peace treaty was signed in November 2016.

In April 2018, the United States updated their joint doctrine on counterinsurgency. The new definition of insurgency drew the US military away from seeing insurgency as targeting one existing 'constituted government' towards a more international, globalised view. 'Insurgency is the organized use of subversion and violence to seize, nullify, or challenge political control of a region. An insurgency is a form of intrastate conflict, and counterinsurgency is used to counter it' (*Joint Publication 3-24*, p.I-1). This new definition has, therefore, followed from experiences in Iraq, Afghanistan and more recently in Syria, Yemen, Ukraine and Palestine. In each of these cases, there has been an international dimension to the insurgency, either through external support, such as the involvement of *Tehrik-i-Taliban Pakistan* (TTP – the Pakistani wing of the Taliban) in the war in Afghanistan, or the Islamic State's ambition to establish a global caliphate. The new definition also accepted that the areas insurgents target may be lacking in formal civil authorities. While these features may not be present in all insurgencies, some theorists, such as Robert Thompson in *Defeating Communist Insurgency* (1966), have seen external support as a critical factor in defining the outcome of a campaign. Indeed, many of the examples used in this book involve some degree of external support.

One final definition is worthy of reference. The Australian counterinsurgency doctrine of 2009 states that insurgency is 'a conflict between opposing parties where at least one is a state actor, in which the catalyst for conflict is a competition of wills' (Australian Army, *Land Warfare Doctrine LWD 3-0-1*, p.1–2). Later definitions have moved away from emphasising state control, but the reference to a Clausewitzian competition of wills is useful. Bringing together the different elements of the UK, US and Australian military definitions of insurgency, a reasonable hybrid can be formulated that strikes a balance between the broad brushstrokes of Clausewitz's definition of war and the more specific character of an insurgency within that. Thus, this volume defines insurgency as:

> An organised use of violence to seize, nullify, or challenge political control of a region. It is a competition of wills. The violence may vary from small-scale ambushes, guerrilla warfare and terrorism to full-scale conventional operations.

By reflecting on the variety of ways insurgent groups use violence, the erroneous notion that insurgency is 'low intensity' or does not involve conventional operations, nor encompass civil war, has been challenged. This definition also avoids the use of the term 'irregular warfare'. The relational nature of that term makes it problematic, although it is commonly used in the literature. The implication of the term is that 'regular war' is conventional state-on-state conflict. This both underappreciates the prevalence of conventional military operations during insurgencies, as well as the frequency of insurgencies as opposed to other types of war.

With a definition of insurgency established, it is now possible to offer a definition of its counter:

> Counterinsurgency is a violent intervention conducted to defeat an insurgency either locally, regionally or internationally. This may rely on a combination of political, military, legal, psychological, social, civic or economic means. Successful counterinsurgency requires an effective understanding of the character of the opposing insurgency and an understanding of how the insurgents are seen domestically and internationally.

Counterinsurgency is therefore defined by its opposition to insurgency. As FM 3-24 notes: 'though insurgency and COIN are two sides of a phenomenon that has been called revolutionary war or internal war they are distinctly different types of operation' (p.12). Any definition of counterinsurgency must, therefore, also recognise the wide field of civil, military and political involvement required. Furthermore, if a counterinsurgency effort is to be successful, it requires a reasonable understanding of both the insurgents' political aims (even if these are multi-faceted) and how they are perceived. The labelling and perceptions of insurgents as terrorists, radicals, bandits, criminals, freedom fighters or rebels has had varying effects on counterinsurgency campaigns. As Richard English recognised regarding terrorism: 'it is probably one of the most powerfully condemnatory words in the English language' (English, *Terrorism*, p.19). Yet the term has been used in a many different contexts to refer to a wide range of actions. Terrorists, guerrillas and insurgents have frequently been treated as one and the same. In Malaya, the British labelled insurgents of the Malayan Communist Party (MCP) and its related offshoots such as the *Min Yuen* as 'bandits' or 'Communist Terrorists'. These terms were only partially accurate. The MCP and *Min Yuen* certainly engaged in actions reasonably defined as terrorism. They combined this with military action against British and Commonwealth forces. Jungle ambushes were a common threat. The MCP attempted to establish political structures and were led by a Central Committee headed by Chin Peng. This ambiguity in terms complicates the approach required for a counterinsurgent force. Terrorism and guerrilla warfare may require different methods to combat them effectively. A varying balance between military activity, intelligence gathering and civilian policing may be required. It is, therefore, worthwhile briefly differentiating some of these terms.

Bard O'Neill's 2002 foreword to Robert Taber's classic 1965 study of Maoist insurgency, *The War of the Flea*, offers a good starting point:

> Terrorism is the threat or use of physical coercion against non-combatants to create fear in order to achieve political objectives. Guerrilla warfare, by contrast, consists of hit-and-run attacks against police and military and

the physical infrastructure that supports them. Insurgents may opt for one or both forms of warfare and in some cases, might even choose to carry out conventional attacks with regular troop formations. (Bard O'Neill, 'Foreword' in Robert Taber, *The War of the Flea*, p.ix)

The fundamental difference for O'Neill is the target and purpose. But problems arise in defining who precisely is a combatant and non-combatant. The murder of Royal Fusilier drummer Lee Rigby near the Royal Artillery Barracks, Woolwich, in London by Michael Adebolajo and Michael Adebowale sits within a grey area. Rigby was targeted as a British soldier by the perpetrators, but he was off-duty and out of uniform at the time of the attack. There is no easy divide in such cases. The conviction of the pair for murder rather than terror offences adds a further layer of complexity when categorising such actions. Terrorists themselves frequently do not make distinctions between combatant and non-combatant. As Shiraz Maher has recognised in his ground-breaking 2016 study *Salafi-Jihadism*: 'the definition of non-combatant is constructed through narrow strictures, while those who can be classed as combatants – or at least, considered legitimate targets – are conceived of in the broadest brush strokes' (Maher, *Salafi-Jihadism*, p.49). Thus, while combatant/non-combatant remains a useful generalisation it should be used with some caution.

The purpose and importance of instilling fear through violence is a significant component of differentiating terrorists from guerrillas, but this too needs some clarification. Terrorist acts are not always solely directed at the targeted population but may also generate support for the cause from external audiences sympathetic to the terrorist organisation's aims. Insurgents hold no monopoly on the use of terror. In Malaya, the British discovered the location of a local communist leader Liu Kon Kim, and after his targeted assassination by men of the Suffolk Regiment, he was paraded around the local villages on the front of a Malayan Police Land Rover. This served the dual purpose of reinforcing British authority and demonstrating the diminishing power of the Malayan communists. This was a small part of what the historian David French described as the 'exemplary use of force' (French, *The British Way*, p.105). This was a common form of coercion throughout Britain's wars of decolonisation. Exemplary force could involve collective punishments, cordon and search operations, the destruction of property, mass arrests, collective fines or curfews. In August 1952, the Malayan village of Permatang Tinggi was burnt down after the villagers refused to cooperate with enquiries into a murdered government official. In more recent times, states have colluded in supporting acts of terror. In September 1991, the academic and critic of apartheid Adrian Guelke was shot by members of the Ulster Freedom Fighters, a loyalist paramilitary group in Northern Ireland. Elements of the South African Defence Force had falsely tipped off the UFF that Guelke was colluding with the nationalist Provisional Irish Republican Army. Guelke survived when two of the guns jammed. This all amounts to a complex, overlapping group of terms; the uses of which must be seen within the context of individual campaigns and taking account of the different perspectives. Definitions are necessary for any counterinsurgent force, but theoretical classifications can only be taken so far. In the end, there will always be a messy overlap between the theories used to describe counterinsurgency and the practice on the ground. This is the central theme of the book. Theory can only offer an abstracted rationalisation of what is a murky, reactive, complex and parlous form of warfare. By exploring this discord, we hope to leave the reader with a deeper understanding of counterinsurgency.

Timeline

1830–47	French conquest of Algeria.
1895–98	Spanish war in Cuba.
1899–1902	South African War.
1899–1902	US war in the Philippines.
1916–18	Arab Revolt against the Ottoman Empire.
1919–21	Irish War of Independence.
1936–39	Arab Revolt.
1944–48	Jewish insurgency in Mandatory Palestine.
1948–60	Malayan Emergency.
1954–62	France's Algerian War.
1952–60	Emergency in Kenya.
1954–75	Vietnam War.
1955–59	Emergency in Cyprus.
1961–74	Angolan War of Independence.
1969	The 'Troubles' begin in Northern Ireland.
2001	11 September attack on the USA. Led to first airstrikes in Afghanistan from October.
2003	Operation *Iraqi Freedom*.
2011	Formation of Free Syrian Army.

CHAPTER 1

The Roots of Counterinsurgency

The Origins of 'Small War'

Guerrilla warfare, if understood as a set of tactics employed by the weak versus the strong, is as old as warfare itself. The same might be said of insurgency (and, thus, counterinsurgency). However, we also need to understand the context in which the phenomena of modern insurgency and counterinsurgency came into being; going back to ancient or medieval history in search of timeless principles of insurgency or counterinsurgency risks distorting our understanding of both.

In European history, the modern state, and the 'regular' armies with which states prosecuted their wars, emerged in the early modern period. However, European wars were not only fought by regular armies but also by partisans and light troops, in what was referred to as 'small war' (*kleine kriege* or *petite guerre*). As European armies increasingly conducted their wars overseas, the raising and employment of irregular forces (usually indigenous levies) increased. For example, in the Seven Years' War (1756–63), British and French irregulars fought each other in North America, while in Europe, Austrian and Russian irregular cavalry (most notably Cossacks in the latter case) fought against the Prussians. Irregular forces were also a common feature of the frontier warfare between the Austrian, Russian and Ottoman Empires.

Many historians have seen the late 18th and early 19th centuries as representing a sea change in the conduct of war in the Western world. In the American War of Independence (1775–83), the Continental Army of the nascent United States played a crucial role in securing victory. However, success also depended on the militia, which was able to harass British lines of communications. The operations of a 'regular' army, therefore, took place alongside a guerrilla conflict, with both forming part of the wider revolutionary struggle for independence. In the French Revolutionary War (1792–1802), France unleashed the full force of 'people's war' in order to defend itself. The *levée en masse* (1793) used the language of total war to mobilise the people and resources of the French state.

In practice, the number of troops put into the field by France was not as impressive as the paper strength of over one million men in arms, but the importance of the *levée en masse* lay more in its rhetoric. Significantly, it applied to internal as much to external threats: an uprising in the Vendée (1793–94) was brutally crushed. During the Napoleonic Wars (1803–15), the logic of people's war would be turned against Napoleon's empire. During the Peninsular War (1807–14), the Spanish launched *La Guerrilla* (small war) against the French occupation, from which the modern term 'guerrilla' is derived. The revolutionary wars of the late 18th and early 19th centuries were crucial in heralding the era of people's war. However, it is important to note that alongside the guerrilla campaign, the Spanish war effort also involved semi-regular and regular Royal Army units, and the lines between the different elements were somewhat fluid.

The major conflicts of the 19th century demonstrated the power of the forces of nationalism and people's war. The American Civil War (1861–65) was an insurgency, in which a total of 11 states seceded from the Union, forming a new nation that would safeguard slavery. It featured regular operations and large-scale pitched battles, as well as low-level guerrilla violence. As Daniel Sutherland has noted, a romanticised view of partisan activity in the War of Independence played a central role in the way that guerrilla conflict was understood in 1861 (Sutherland, *A Savage Conflict*, 2009, pp.9–11). The prominence of guerrilla warfare, the scale of the conflict and its increasing totality, and the demands of reoccupying the seceded states meant the Union was forced to define the differences between soldiers, partisans, brigands and civilians, and to establish rules of conduct. The result was General Orders (G.O.) No. 100, otherwise known as the Lieber Code (April 1863). Articles 81 and 82 noted:

> Partisans are soldiers armed and wearing the uniform of their army, but belonging to a corps which acts detached from the main body for the purpose of making inroads into the territory occupied by the enemy. If captured, they are entitled to all the privileges of the prisoner of war.

> Men, or squads of men, who commit hostilities, whether by fighting, or inroads for destruction or plunder, or by raids of any kind, without commission, without being part and portion of the organized hostile army, and without sharing continuously in the war, but who do so with intermitting returns to their homes and avocations, or with the occasional assumption of the semblance of peaceful pursuits, divesting themselves of the character or appearance of soldiers – such men, or squads of men, are not public enemies, and, therefore, if captured, are not entitled to the privileges of prisoners of war, but shall be treated summarily as highway robbers or pirates.

The Union increasingly fought a 'hard war' against the Confederacy's population, most notably in Union Major-General William T. Sherman's march to the sea (November–December 1864) and through the Carolinas in 1865. Guerrilla warfare also exposed some of the cracks in Southern society: in many states, anti-war or pro-Union groups took up arms. The Confederate leadership – Robert E. Lee in particular – generally saw the guerrilla campaign as merely an adjunct to regular operations. Lee's surrender at Appomattox on 9 April 1865 was crucial: Confederate troops stood down, rather than melting into the countryside to fight an extended guerrilla war.

In Europe, the largest conflict between 1815 and 1914 was the Franco-Prussian War (1870–71). Following the defeat of the regular French army in 1870, there was a second phase of 'people's war', which saw a *levée en masse* of the French population and partisan activity by *francs-tireurs* against Prussian forces. The war, therefore, also demonstrated the powerful forces that could be unleashed within a nation at arms.

Small Wars for Empire

The expansion of European empires was both a cause and a result of imperial wars of conquest. These were often followed by 'pacification' campaigns, in which European armies developed their counterinsurgency practices. In the colonial context, the term 'small war' is a Eurocentric one, suggestive of a war of lesser importance, a conflict on the periphery, where European armies could get away with much more than they could in Europe. For European militaries, colonial wars were limited in terms of ends and means, but they often tended towards totality for native populations. The colonial environment also saw the emergence of many of the most frequently cited theorists of counterinsurgency.

In Britain, the term 'small wars' became commonplace, widely used to describe imperial campaigns against non-European opponents. If 'regular' warfare was the European warfare of the period (such as the Franco-Prussian War), small wars were those that the British fought to defend or further their imperial interests. As Byron Farwell has written, 'there was not a single year in Queen Victoria's long reign [1837–1901] in which somewhere in the world her soldiers were not fighting for her and for her empire' (Farwell, *Queen Victoria's Little Wars*, p.1). The British fought only one war against a European power between 1815 and 1914: the Crimean War against Russia (1853–56, with British participation from 1854). The rest were all wars of empire.

The British, therefore, gained extensive experience in the 'art' of small wars. Many British commentators perceived that they faced very different strategic problems to those faced by the other Great Powers. In the period 1815 to 1945, the European powers maintained large (usually conscript) armies. Britain was an island nation with a global maritime empire; the security of which rested on a large navy and an expeditionary (and usually small) army. The army needed to be ready for a possible major European war, but it also needed to be ready to fight small wars, and increasingly (after the British Empire reached the zenith of its territorial extent in 1919), it needed to be able to wage counterinsurgency campaigns against colonial insurgencies. Field Service Regulations (FSR) 1930 noted that 'the British Empire is confronted with problems peculiarly its own' (pp.1–2). Hew Strachan has pointed out that the main cultural determinant of the British army was not the relationship between maritime power and military power, but between big wars (regular or conventional conflicts) and small wars (Strachan, *Big Wars and Small Wars*, p.6).

In the English language, the most extensive codification of the principles of colonial warfare as they stood at the turn of the century was the soldier and writer Charles E. Callwell (1859–1928). His *Small Wars: Their Principles and Practice* (1896) was published as a semi-official manual. He reached the rank of major-general following a long career that included service in the South African War (1899–1902). Callwell recognised the weaknesses of his definition that small wars included 'all campaigns other than those where both the opposing sides consist of regular troops' and accepted that the expression was used 'in default of a better'. Indeed, small wars were often anything but 'small', the South African War being a prime example (Callwell, *Small Wars*, pp.21–22).

Callwell is sometimes seen as the first author in the British counterinsurgency canon. However, he was not a theorist of counterinsurgency as we would now understand the term. He divided small wars into three classes: wars of conquest, pacification campaigns and campaigns to wipe out an insult, avenge a wrong or overthrow a dangerous enemy. Only the second category could be described as related to modern-day counterinsurgency. Moreover, he believed that 'irregular' warfare should be kept as 'regular' as possible: 'The whole spirit of the art of conducting small wars,' he wrote, 'is to strive for the attainment of decisive methods', which meant victory on the battlefield (Ibid, p.125). The alternative was a long, drawn-out guerrilla war.

Of pacification operations, Callwell wrote that 'As a general rule the quelling of rebellion in distant colonies means protracted, thankless, invertebrate war' (Ibid, p.27). He quoted Field Marshal Sir Garnet Wolseley, whom he believed had put it best in his famous *Soldier's Pocket Book for Field Service* (1869). 'In planning a war against an uncivilised nation who have perhaps no capital,' Wolseley wrote, 'your first object should be the capture of whatever they prize most, and the destruction or deprivation of which will probably bring the war most rapidly to a conclusion' (Ibid, p.40). Ultimately, this logic justified 'butcher and bolt' methods: the destruction of the enemy's villages and food supplies in order to bring them to heel. Exemplary force was, therefore, entirely justifiable in Callwell's vision of counterinsurgency. Violence would generate a 'moral effect', the all-importance of which was a recurring theme in small wars literature. Callwell set this theme out early in *Small Wars*: 'moral effect,' he wrote, 'is often far more important than material success' (Ibid, p.42).

Callwell's work is often a starting point for historians examining the conduct of small wars. Several noteworthy principles stand out. Callwell repeatedly compared small and 'regular' warfare. Fighting small wars might have been 'in certain respects an art by itself', but there were still 'points which permit comparisons to be established' (Ibid, p.23). He also stressed that small wars were difficult and victory on the battlefield was not to be taken for granted. While we cannot avoid his assumption of European superiority, Callwell realised the technological gap between regular and irregular forces was closing. He also contended that small wars were as much 'campaigns against nature' (Ibid, p.44) as they were against the irregular opposition. Climate, terrain, and disease all presented huge problems, and the regular forces were usually chained to long, vulnerable lines of communication. Logistics exercised a dominating effect over strategy; the army often became 'a mere escort for its food' (Ibid, p.59). Gathering solid intelligence (on both the enemy and the theatre of war) was difficult and needed to be prioritised. For all these reasons, Callwell emphasised the importance of having a plan and carrying it through.

The French army also gained extensive experience of colonial warfare, and those usually referenced with regard to small wars are Marshals Thomas-Robert Bugeaud (1784–1849), Joseph Galliéni (1849–1916), and Hubert Lyautey (1854–1934). The French conquest of Algeria (1830–47) involved an extensive pacification campaign. Appointed to command in December 1840, Bugeaud employed the 'razzia' (raid) as his preferred tactical method. 'Razzia' was a term borrowed from Algeria, but the concept behind its use by the French army was a European 'small wars' one. Bugeaud recognised the difficulty that the regular army faced: 'In Europe, we don't just make war against armies, we make war against interests', he said in a speech in 1840. 'But there are no equivalent interests to seize in Algeria, or at least there's only one, the agricultural interest' (Thoral, 'French Colonial Counter-Insurgency', pp.16–17). Moreover, the enemy did not fight as one army that could be brought to battle and defeated. In order to win, it was necessary for the regular troops to disperse. Raids would allow the regulars to strike directly at the enemy's interests and generate moral effect. The army's methods were often brutal: as the historian and political thinker Alexis de Tocqueville (1805–59) opined, 'In the interest of France's glory and reputation in Europe, the French must accept the violence and expense necessary to establish a permanent French presence in North Africa' (Gallois, 'Dahra', in Martin Thomas (ed.), *The French Colonial Mind, Volume 2*, p.5). Perhaps the most notorious example was *enfumade*, in which the French started fires in order to 'smoke out' Algerians from their cave hideouts, or indeed, to asphyxiate them. The most famous example was Colonel Jean Jacques Pélissier's attack on the Ouled Riah in their caves in the Dahra mountains in June 1845, from which some 600 bodies were recovered, the vast majority of them dead. Bugeaud also recognised the importance of colonial development, and he reorganised the *bureaux arabes*, which administered the country. Bugeaud departed in July 1846, and in 1848, Alger (Algiers), Constantine and Oran were established as *départements* of France.

Galliéni is more famous for the battle of the Marne in 1914, but he spent most of his career abroad. In 1892, he was sent to French Indochina, and in 1896, he took command of the French expedition to Madagascar. He stayed there as Governor-General until 1905. Lyautey was very much Galliéni's protégé: he served under him in Indochina from 1894, then in Madagascar between 1897 and 1902, and later commanded French troops in Morocco. In Indochina, Galliéni put into practice what he called 'progressive occupation', where bases were established from which patrols would extend the area of control. Lyautey acted as the codifier of principles when he set out his views in an important article, 'Du rôle colonial de l'Armée', published in *Revue des Deux Mondes* in 1900. Lyautey had called for officers to have a 'social role', and the empire appeared to offer that opportunity. He argued that the colonial army became 'an organization on the march'. 'A colonial soldier was more than a warrior,' as Douglas Porch put it. 'He was an administrator, farmer, architect, and engineer – in short, he took up any skill required to develop the region in his charge' (Porch, 'Bugeaud, Galliéni, Lyautey', in Paret (ed.), *Makers of Modern Strategy*, p.390). However, the army's colonial role was also linked to France's *mission civilisatrice* (civilising mission); the sort of language that would have been familiar to Callwell. Indeed, Porch concluded that Lyautey's approach was 'more a public-relations exercise' to sell empire to the French (Ibid, pp.394–395), while Michael Finch notes the Galliéni method 'was governed by his understanding of war and enacted within a colonial framework which accepted far greater levels of violence than could be tolerated today' (Finch, *A Progressive Occupation*, p.236).

The **tâche d'huile ('oil spot') method** describes a method of pacification in which the occupied zone is methodically expanded outwards from its bases, rather like an oil slick. Military occupation included political, social and economic development to win over the population, or at least to separate them from insurgent fighters. The method proved influential: the central idea has been implemented in numerous counterinsurgency campaigns, and modern-day counterinsurgency works still reference it.

We can see in the development of this body of writing what Finch has called a 'sideways spread of influence, whereby colonial forces might learn from each other' (Finch, *A Progressive Occupation*, p.228). For example, Callwell applied lessons from the colonial wars of other countries, particularly France and Russia. He particularly praised Bugeaud for his understanding of small wars. On the other hand, *Small Wars* was translated into French. The emergence of a common set of principles is best demonstrated by looking at three case studies from colonial wars that took place around the same time: the Spanish war in Cuba (1895–98), the South African War (1899–1902), and the US war in the Philippines (1899–1902).

Perhaps the most notorious measure to emerge was the use of concentration camps. The term 'concentration camp' has become so heavily associated with Nazism that there is the potential for confusion, given the different purposes of the camps in, for example, South Africa. Indeed, André Wessels has suggested that the term 'internment camp' might be adopted, in order to better convey the different purposes of the camps in South Africa (Wessels, 'Boer Guerrilla and British Counter-Guerrilla', p.13). Nor did the British invent the term, or the concept, as is often believed. The Spanish referred to *Reconcentración* and *concentrados* (concentrated peoples) in their war in Cuba (1895–98).

The European powers made extensive use of **concentration camps** in their colonial wars. The Spanish, Americans and British all used reconcentration in their colonial conflicts of the 1890s, in which the purpose was to separate enemy fighters from the population. Although not to be confused with Nazi concentration camps, death rates were still high owing to disease, maladministration and neglect. An estimated 40,000–60,000 people died in the British camps in the South African War (1899–1902).

Captain-General Valeriano Weyler (1838–1930) was appointed to command Spanish forces in 1896, part of a concerted effort to intensify the war. His is the name most associated with the camp policy: one of his first decrees was to order the concentration of the rural population in the eastern part of the island, a measure that was eventually extended to cover the western and central provinces as well. There was little attempt to win 'hearts and minds' here. An estimated 170,000 internees died in the concentration centres. As Iain Smith and Andreas Stucki note, in military terms, the policy was a success, but in political terms, it was unacceptable to Spain's new liberal government (which came to power in autumn 1897) and to the USA (Smith and Stucki, 'The Colonial Development of Concentration Camps', p.423).

The South African War (1899–1902) was the largest of Britain's small wars. It required the use of some 450,000 British and imperial troops. Of these, 5,774 were killed in action and 22,829 were wounded. A further 16,168 died of wounds, disease or in accidents. Total casualties (including those who fell sick) were in excess of a hundred thousand. The cost to the taxpayer was more than £200 million. The South African War warrants inclusion here because the Boers used guerrilla warfare extensively. It also offers a good example of the intersection of theory and practice, given that Callwell incorporated the lessons of the South African War into the 1906 edition of *Small Wars*. His contention that the system of large-scale 'drives' to root out Boer commandos represented 'the last word' (Callwell, *Small Wars*, p.143) in counter-guerrilla warfare proved excessively optimistic. The British had not stumbled upon a winning formula. Yet these drives would remain a central part of British counterinsurgency strategy for many years to come.

The war began with a 'conventional' phase in which the Boers got their attacks in first following the expiration of their ultimatum on 11 October 1899. They laid siege to three towns – Ladysmith, Kimberley, and Mafeking – which forced the British to launch relief operations. The result was a famous series of defeats, at Stormberg (10 December), Magersfontein (11 December) and Colenso (15 December), known cumulatively as 'black week'. However, by getting bogged down in siege warfare, the Boers allowed the British to wrest back the initiative. The siege of Ladysmith was relieved by General Sir Redvers Buller in February 1900. Field Marshal Lord Roberts invaded the Orange Free State (lifting the siege of Kimberley in the process) and occupied its capital, Bloemfontein, on 13 March 1900. The relief of Mafeking in May set off wild celebrations in Britain. The British marched into Pretoria, the capital of the Transvaal, on 5 June 1900. Both Boer states were annexed. Roberts believed that the war was over, and returned home in November 1900. As Wessels has noted, Roberts had turned the tide but not won decisive victory, and 'in practice the British were only in control of the (former) republics as far as their guns could shoot' (Wessels, 'Boer Guerrilla and British Counter-Guerrilla', p.9).

Indeed, a new phase of the struggle had already begun. Shortly after the fall of Bloemfontein, a *krijgsraad* (war council) was held at Kroonstad on 17 March 1900, which made the decision to change tack. Instead of taking up defensive positions across a broad front, republican forces would be organised into smaller, more mobile units, which would concentrate on attacking the British lines of communication and harassing British forces wherever possible. The objective was to prolong the conflict to achieve a more favourable peace settlement. As Wessels has noted, it is ironic that it was only now that the Boers started to exploit their chief strength against a conventional army, namely mobility. Moreover, the more conservative Boer commanders were being replaced by more adventurous leaders like Christiaan de Wet, Koos de la Rey, and Louis Botha.

In Britain, de Wet became the most famous guerrilla commander, thanks to repeated failed efforts to catch him. De Wet wrote in his account, *Three Years War* (1902), that 'To oppose successfully such bodies of men as our burghers had to meet during this war demanded *rapidity of action* more than anything else. We had to be quick at fighting, quick at reconnoitring, quick (if it became necessary) at flying! This was exactly what I myself aimed at' (De Wet, *Three Years War*, p.99). This was a strategy of the weak, as he recognised: 'How, then, could we think of making a stand, with our tiny forces, against two hundred and forty thousand men, with three or four hundred guns? All we could do was to make the best of every little chance we got of hampering the enemy. If fortune should desert us, it only remained to flee' (Ibid, p.118). Notably, de Wet argued the Boers continued to fight for their legitimate governments and, therefore, they were not 'guerrillas'; a term he associated with banditry.

In response, the British employed a range of counter-guerrilla methods, which began under Roberts and intensified under his replacement General Horatio Herbert Kitchener. Many violated accepted norms of war. However, the same rules did not apply in small wars. The Boers were a white opponent but were not seen as wholly civilised: 'These boers [*sic*] are uncivilized Africander [*sic*] savages with only a thin white veneer,' Kitchener wrote to Brodrick, the Secretary of State for War, on 21 June 1901 (Wessels (ed.), *Lord Kitchener*, p.130). First, the British used mobile columns. Mounted infantry was crucial. The more mobile the British forces became, the more they were able to neutralise (at least to some extent) the Boers' initial mobility advantage, although coordinating the movements of separated columns across difficult country proved challenging. In spite of this, de Wet evaded capture in the so-called 'de Wet hunts', although he was put under pressure, especially in the third or 'great' hunt of January–March 1901. The British could also make use of the mobility provided by railways, although here the obvious limitations were that Boers could ride where trains could not, and railways were often overtaxed. Complementing this was the development of static defences: blockhouses and barbed wire were used to control the countryside. Lines of blockhouses generally followed the railways but also divided up the open spaces of the South African veld. By the end of the war, there were 8,000 blockhouses and 6,000 km of barbed wire. All of this required huge numbers of men, mostly for garrison duty. In May 1901, Kitchener commanded a peak of 240,000 troops. The British made use of irregular forces, either formed in South Africa or consisting of volunteers from colonies, such as Australia and New Zealand, and also used over 100,000 black Africans in various roles (such as scouting or as labourers), many of whom were armed.

Even this elaborate network of blockhouses was by no means watertight. The British, therefore, employed scorched-earth tactics: if the Boers could not be caught, the British sought to deny them food and shelter through destruction of farms and livestock. The first farm burnings occurred at an early stage of the war, and Boer farms increasingly came to be seen as legitimate military targets. By stripping the land, the British hoped to undermine their adversaries' ability and will to fight on. As S. B. Spies noted, the strategy was 'deliberate, massive, widespread and ruthless' (Spies, *Methods of Barbarism*, p.122). Many properties were destroyed for no other reason than their owners were away fighting the British ('on commando'). More than 100,000 buildings were destroyed in total, including more than 40 towns and villages. Scorched-earth was heavily criticised, but it contributed considerably to the war of attrition.

Complementing scorched-earth was the most infamous measure: the use of concentration camps. Kitchener issued a circular on 21 December 1900 in which he stated his desire to stop guerrilla warfare by bringing in women and children. He believed that

Boer women were keeping their men in the war and wished to separate the guerrillas from the population (Wessels (ed.), *Lord Kitchener*, p.60). The camps began as a temporary measure but soon became part of the wider counterinsurgency strategy. We know much more about the 'white' camps than we do about the 'black' ones. Conditions in both cases were appalling. The camps were located near to railways in order to ease supply problems, but sites were often poorly chosen, basic hygiene was lacking and administration was poor. The result was that logistics broke down, leading to starvation, and disease ran rampant. A measles epidemic in 1901 proved particularly devastating to a population that had low immunity to the disease. Smith and Stucki estimate that at least 40,000 died in total; Wessels estimated 50,000–60,000 (Smith and Stucki, 'The Colonial Development of Concentration Camps', p.427; Wessels, 'Boer Guerrilla and British Counter-Guerrilla', p.13). 'I wish I could get rid of all these camps,' Kitchener wrote to Brodrick on 9 May 1901, 'but it is the only way to settle the country and enable the men to leave their commandos and come in to their families without being caught and tried for desertion' (Wessels (ed.), *Lord Kitchener*, p.113). Emily Hobhouse's 1901 report on severity of the camps generated considerable controversy. British measures were famously denounced in a speech by the Liberal leader, Sir Henry Campbell-Bannerman, on 14 June 1901: 'When is a war not a war?,' he asked, 'When it is carried on by methods of barbarism in South Africa' (Spies, *Methods of Barbarism*, p.1). Because of such criticisms, the government sent a Commission of Enquiry under Millicent Garrett Fawcett. Their recommendations formed an important part of the process of reform, in which mortality figures were brought under control. Smith and Stucki conclude that 'The deaths of all those Boer civilians in British camps, especially of women and children, were unintended but they were deaths all the same, and they have cast a long shadow over Boer-British relations ever since' (Smith and Stucki, 'The Colonial Development of Concentration Camps', p.431).

The British also employed psychological warfare. They sought to induce guerrillas to surrender, or issued threats: such as a proclamation in June 1900 declaring that when a railway line was attacked the houses in the vicinity would be burnt down, or Kitchener's proclamation of 7 August 1901 threatening to banish those who did not surrender by 15 September 1901. Boers who remained in the field generally treated these proclamations with contempt.

Indeed, destruction of Boer farms and the removal of families to the camps could increase the sense that there was nothing to lose. To that end, the British decision to leave women and children in the open after destroying their farms played a role in hastening the end of the war. Moreover, the British efforts to encourage Boers to throw in the towel did bear fruit; the some 5,500 'joiners', Boers who joined the British side, became a crucial part of the British intelligence effort, and their participation on the British side was profoundly demoralising to the Boer 'bitter enders'. Indeed, de Wet later maintained that the Boers lost the war because 'so many of our burghers proved false to their own colours' (De Wet, *Three Years War*, p.99). The Boer attempt to spread the war to the Cape Colony, and to encourage Cape Afrikaners to rally to their cause, was partly stifled by the deployment of large numbers of British troops and by the use of martial law; 44 Cape rebels were executed (although 391 had their death sentences commuted).

These ingredients came together when British forces sought to 'drive' guerrillas against blockhouse lines. The idea culminated in the so-called 'new-model drives' that Kitchener launched against de Wet from 5 February to 8 May 1902. These large-scale operations involved a line of British troops moving forwards and 'driving' Boer guerrillas onto the blockhouse lines, where they could be captured. The results were not always as hoped, but these new methods were systematic and helped to drain away what was left of Boer ability and will to resist any longer. The Peace of Vereeniging was signed on 31 May 1902. Attrition had done its work. Guerrilla numbers were dwindling, and with no external intervention in sight, there was no prospect of victory. The plight of women and children was a major concern, the spectre of race war loomed and it was felt that British terms were more generous than they would be if the war continued for much longer.

The United States faced a similar campaign in the Philippines (1899–1902). The Spanish war in Cuba formed a justification for American intervention and what became the Spanish-American War of 1898. The war opened the door to US involvement in the Philippines: the US Navy's victory over the Spanish at the battle of Manila Bay (1 May 1898) was decisive, and the US seized the opportunity by dispatching a military expedition. Brian M. Linn, in his book *The Philippine War* (2000), describes what followed as a 'disordered leap toward empire' (Linn, *The Philippine War*, p.7). The first US troops arrived at the end of June. On 12 June, the Philippines had declared its independence, and Emilio Aguinaldo (1869–1964) was chosen as President. However, in the battle of Manila (13 August 1898), the Spanish surrendered and handed the city to US troops. Linn argues that in failing to join the attack, Aguinaldo made a crucial error (Ibid, p.25). In the second battle of Manila (4–5 February 1899), US troops under Major-General Elwell S. Otis defeated the Filipino Army of Liberation in what was to be the biggest battle of the war, taking 238 casualties in the process. Army of Liberation losses were reckoned to be 4,000. At the end of February, US forces defeated an uprising in Manila and an attempted counterattack by the Army of Liberation. Otis then launched a series of campaigns that aimed to destroy the Army of Liberation and capture Aguinaldo. These were generally successful, albeit without destroying Filipino resistance or capturing the President.

Aguinaldo's initial strategy included guerrilla warfare, but only as a last resort; with the defeat of the Army of Liberation in 'regular' engagements, the Filipino leader was left with no alternative. On 13 November 1899, Aguinaldo decided to move to guerrilla warfare. Otis, who was replaced by Major-General Arthur MacArthur in May 1900, was convinced that the war was virtually over. He was wrong, much as Roberts had been in South Africa. The war posed a formidable logistical challenge, and the US had to deal with the problem of an unfriendly population. Linn suggests the zenith for the guerrillas in this regard came at the start of 1900, and the support they enjoyed declined thereafter (Ibid, pp.196–197). Otis divided the country into four departments, each divided into districts and sub-districts. The policy of President William McKinley (1897–1901) was described by Stuart Creighton Miller as one of 'benevolent assimilation, substituting the mild sway of justice and right for arbitrary rule' (Miller, *Benevolent Assimilation*, p.ii), and many believed the Filipinos would welcome the benefits of US imperialism.

However, there was plenty of 'stick' to accompany the 'carrot'. The defeat of Filipino resistance in 1901, seen as the 'year of victory' by John M. Gates (*Schoolbooks and Krags*, pp.225–247), was the result of military campaigns that ended resistance in 21 of the 38 unpacified provinces. Aguinaldo was captured in March 1901 in a daring raid led by Colonel Frederick Funston, although this did not end the war. In July 1901, MacArthur was replaced as commander by Major-General Adna R. Chaffee. US forces began to use sweeps far more effectively, intelligence improved and punitive measures were used to quell resistance. Linn notes that the power to retaliate was permitted under G.O. 100 and international military law, but there were wide variations in how officers chose to enforce this power. For example, the relocation of much of Batangas's civilian population to concentration camps proved controversial. Commentators, especially in the press, were aware of what had been happening elsewhere. As Miller notes in his *Benevolent Assimilation* (1982), many newspapers criticised 'Weylerism' and the 'Kitchener Plan' (Miller, *Benevolent Assimilation*, pp.163, 208–209, 228–229).

The most infamous events occurred on the island of Samar. On 28 September 1901, townspeople and guerrillas attacked the US garrison at Balangiga, killing 48 officers and men. This became known as the 'Balangiga massacre'. The US response was swift and brutal. The 6th Separate Brigade was created, and Chaffee appointed Brigadier-General Jacob H. Smith to command it. This was, as Linn points out, a bad mistake: Smith was temperamentally unsuited to the job (Linn, *The Philippine War*, p.312). Marine Major Littleton

W. T. Waller was given an unsigned, handwritten note from Smith ordering that his men should 'make the interior of Samar a howling wilderness' (Miller, *Benevolent Assimilation*, p.222). Between 31 October and 10 November 1901, Waller's expedition burned 255 houses and killed 39 men, as well as destroying one ton of hemp, half a ton of rice and 30 boats. They then launched a disastrous march from Lanang to Basey (28 December 1901–19 January 1902), and executed 12 civilians at Basey. Waller was subsequently court-martialled for murder. The trial, and his subsequent acquittal, caused controversy. In his defence, Waller claimed that G.O. 100 permitted his methods. Smith was also court-martialled and found guilty of 'conduct to the prejudice of good order and military discipline'. Linn argues that Samar became established in public memory as being representative of the conduct of the whole war but suggests it was far more complex and challenging than superficial narratives allow, although he notes that the army's reputation had been tarnished (Linn, *The Philippine War*, pp.321, 328).

The Age of 'Imperial Policing'

The upheavals produced by World War I (1914–18) included the collapse of four great empires: Imperial Germany, Austria-Hungary, the Ottoman Empire and Tsarist Russia. The British and French Empires expanded, but both faced resistance to their imperial rule. The resulting counterinsurgency campaigns could be fought using all the accoutrements of modern, industrial war.

Air power 'came of age' during World War I. Britain's Royal Air Force (RAF), created on 1 April 1918 as the first independent air arm in the world, was available for service in the post-war counterinsurgency campaigns. Air Marshal Sir Hugh Trenchard, Chief of the Air Staff from 1919 to 1930, was certainly eager to seize an appropriate opportunity. Between 1918 and 1939, military aviation became a central component of colonial warfare, with the RAF taking over defence in Mesopotamia, Palestine, Transjordan and Aden. Air control proved largely successful, although it should not be assumed that this proved the possibility of 'victory through air power': success depended on 'boots on the ground', and this was well understood, not least by the airmen themselves.

Britain faced a bewildering array of problems in the aftermath of World War I, such that historians have hailed it as a 'crisis of empire'. First, the heavy spending of the war years meant that greater parsimony in defence spending was required in the post-war period. Second, Britain needed to rapidly demobilise. Third, these financial and manpower constraints affected Britain's ability to deal with a range of security threats across the globe. There was mounting unrest in Ireland, India and Egypt. Britain also needed to police its new territories, such as Palestine. In short, therefore, the British army reverted to its traditional imperial role.

T. E. Lawrence is one of the most famous writers on guerrilla warfare. He is one of those historical figures for whom it becomes difficult to separate the man from the myth, thanks to films such as *Lawrence of Arabia* (1962). Lawrence became a key figure in the Arab Revolt against Ottoman rule (1916–18). After World War I, he told his story in classic books such as *Seven Pillars of Wisdom* (1926) and sought to rationalise what had happened into a 'science' of guerrilla warfare. Lawrence's writings were widely revisited during the counterinsurgency boom of the 2000s. One of his maxims (in particular) seemed to stand out as the US, UK and others became embroiled in wars in 'host nations' such as Iraq: 'Do not try to do too much with your own hands. Better the Arabs do it tolerably than that you do it perfectly. It is their war, and you are to help them, not to win it for them. Actually, also, under the very odd conditions of Arabia, your practical work will not be as good as, perhaps, you think it is' ('Twenty-Seven Articles', Article XV).

The Irish War of Independence

The Irish War of Independence (1919–21) was in many ways Britain's definitive counterinsurgency experience of the inter-war years. It was colonial warfare brought home. Ireland was England's oldest colony, and the conduct of the conflict had much in common with a colonial small war; but since the Act of Union had come into force on 1 January 1801, Ireland was part of the United Kingdom. It was also a civil war. Ireland offered an example of a successful insurgency against an imperial power. Nationalists in India and elsewhere looked on with great interest, and later insurgent groups, such as those of the Jewish insurgency in Mandatory Palestine (1944–48), consciously drew on the Irish example.

It is easy to forget that in July 1914, as Europe spiralled towards war, British eyes were focused on the Ulster Crisis. The issue of Home Rule prompted stiff resistance from Unionists, and the Ulster Volunteer Force (UVF) was formally established in January 1913. The government introduced its Home Rule Bill in April. As the crisis escalated, the nationalists also began arming, forming the Irish Volunteers in November 1913. Historians have noted the significance of the introduction of paramilitary politics, which made violence likely. Had it not been for war in 1914, there might well have been civil war in Ireland. As it was, the Irish Parliamentary Party (IPP), under their leader John Redmond, rallied behind the British war effort. The nationalist Easter Rising of 1916 was not initially popular amongst the Irish and was swiftly crushed by British troops. However, the aftermath saw the British make a crucial error, executing many of the ringleaders by firing squad. The turning point came in 1918. On 21 March 1918, the German army launched its final effort to win the war on the Western Front. In the crisis that followed, the British looked to expand their manpower base as quickly as possible. Conscription had been introduced in Britain in 1916, but Ireland had been excluded. The decision to extend conscription to Ireland, even though it was not implemented, had far-reaching consequences. At the close of the debate in the

Commons on 16 April 1918, the IPP walked out. Indeed, by 1918, Sinn Féin had replaced the IPP as the predominant force in Irish politics. The discontent that the conscription question caused helped to ensure that Britain would face strong nationalist opposition when the war on the Western Front ended on 11 November 1918.

The December 1918 election was a triumph for Sinn Féin. It won 73 seats, while the IPP won only six (with the Unionists winning 26). On 21 January 1919, the first Dáil (parliament) met and issued a declaration of independence. The same day, at Soloheadbeg in Tipperary, a small party of men from the Third Tipperary Brigade, including Dan Breen, Seán Hogan, Seán Treacy and Séamus Robinson, ambushed a consignment of gelignite which was en route to a nearby quarry. Two members of the Royal Irish Constabulary (RIC) escorting it, Patrick MacDonnell and James O'Connell – both Irishmen – were killed. The establishment of the Dáil was a significant event but, although Soloheadbeg is regarded as the opening of the military campaign, this was not so clear at the time. The ambush was the result of a local initiative and the deaths of the two policemen shocked many.

The Volunteers – increasingly referred to as the Irish Republican Army (IRA) in 1919 – were not ready for conflict, and hostilities in 1919 were episodic. Indeed, the Irish War of Independence is best understood as a series of local conflicts, with varying degrees of central control exercised from Dublin. There were significant variations in the levels of violence across Ireland. Tom Barry, who commanded the West Cork Flying Column and later penned the famous account *Guerilla Days in Ireland* (1949), described the conflict as 'a war between the British Army and the Irish people', thereby explaining why the IRA was able to win (p.333). However, the people were by no means universally behind the IRA. As with any insurgency, the objective was to destroy British legitimacy and outlast Britain's will to maintain control. The IRA director of intelligence was Michael Collins (1890–1922), an important figure in the development of modern urban guerrilla warfare, although his ability to control events is often overstated and his role over-emphasised at the expense of leaders at the local level. In February 1919, Collins successfully orchestrated the escape from prison of Eamon de Valera (1882–1975), who was elected President of the Dáil on 1 April.

The British lord lieutenant from 1918 to 1921, Field Marshal Sir John French (1852–1925), pressed for stern measures, including martial law, but this was not politically acceptable in 1919. French would describe the situation in February 1920 as 'something in the nature of an incipient Boer War', and the conflict escalated that summer (Sheehan, *A Hard Local War*, p.94). Parliament passed the Restoration of Order in Ireland Act (ROIA) on 9 August. This permitted the use of more repressive measures, but the Lloyd George government (1916–22) was only belatedly coming to appreciate the nature of the crisis it faced. It was distracted by the difficulties of peace-making and the complex challenges of the post-war world and was reluctant to acknowledge the reality of what was happening in Ireland, while the erratic development of the guerrilla campaign helped to hide the scale of the threat posed by the IRA. Charles Townshend has suggested that ROIA 'confirmed Ireland's separateness from British norms', and the situation in Ireland was neither a time of war nor of peace, as conventionally understood (Townshend, *The Republic*, p.152). For instance, Lloyd George argued 'The Irish job was a policeman's job supported by the military and not vice versa,' and the British, therefore, relied on the RIC to defeat the IRA (Leeson, *Black and Tans*, p.4). However, the IRA focused on the RIC as its primary target. It launched a sustained campaign of intimidation, targeting RIC barracks, as a result of which many outposts were abandoned. The RIC suffered from a manpower shortage as hundreds left the service, on top of losses in action. Between July and September 1920, its strength fell by 1,300. As it was, the RIC's strength was only 9,276 non-commissioned officers and men at the start of 1920. As Andrew Silke has noted, the result was that the RIC became an increasingly alien organisation (Silke, 'Ferocious Times', p.422). In the resulting vacuum, the Dáil was able to establish its own administration. Arguably, the most successful aspect of this parallel administration was the republican justice system, with the courts proving remarkably effective.

The British responded by raising ad hoc irregular forces, the infamous 'Black and Tans', so-called because of the mixture of RIC and military uniform. As D. M. Leeson put it in his book *The Black and Tans* (2011), 'instead of replacing the police with soldiers, the government recruited ex-soldiers to work as police' (p.4). Major-General Henry Hugh Tudor, Police Adviser to the Irish government, also set up the Auxiliary Division of the RIC (ADRIC), known as the 'Auxies'. As the war escalated, the security forces responded to the IRA's activities with their own acts of violence. The Black and Tans, and Auxies, became associated with reprisals and, as Anne Dolan has noted, gained a reputation for violence that far outstripped their numerical significance: 9,000 Black and Tans, and 2,200 Auxies, compared to 60,000 troops (Dolan, 'Paramilitary Violence', in Gerwarth and Horne (eds.), *War in Peace*, p.208). Indeed, the expression 'Tan War' stuck as a term to describe the conflict, and the Black and Tans became a reference point in subsequent debates over Britain's conduct of its counterinsurgency campaigns. It was long assumed that the men who became Black and Tans were former criminals or soldiers who had been brutalised by World War I. However, Leeson has presented a more nuanced picture. 'It was the conditions in which they served,' Leeson wrote, 'rather than their pre-existing dispositions, that drove many Black and Tans to fight terror, as they saw it, with terror.' The chief conditions in question were 'the stresses of counter-revolutionary warfare, compounded by the self-defeating policies of the British government, which sent police to do a job that should have been done either by soldiers or politicians.' He notes that by the time of the truce that brought the shooting to an end, the RIC were a police force in name only and had become an irregular military force (Leeson, *Black and Tans*, pp.2–3, 15–16).

Two notable examples of reprisals occurred on 21 September 1920, when the British sacked the town of Balbriggan, 20 miles north of Dublin, and on 11–12 December 1920, when Cork was set ablaze. Such incidents were not planned and represented what Michael Hopkinson has called a bitter tit-for-tat, in which the actions of one side precipitated reprisals by the other. Equally, they were not random either. Targets were selected in what essentially became, as Leeson puts it, a form of rough justice. Indeed, there were fears that an inability to respond to IRA actions would have an adverse effect on the morale of the police and army. Such reprisals also suggest continuity with the 'butcher and bolt' methods predominant before World War I. As Hopkinson also notes, such measures were ultimately counterproductive, and it was remarkable that the authorities did not realise this sooner (Hopkinson, *Irish War of Independence*, pp.84, 109; Leeson, *Black and Tans*, p.191).

Other incidents in the autumn of 1920 that had a significant impact included the death of the Lord Mayor of Cork, Terence MacSwiney, on the 74th day of a hunger strike (25 October), which made international news. The execution of 18-year-old Kevin Barry, on 1 November, was also controversial. The best-known event of this period of escalation is Bloody Sunday on 21 November 1920. That morning, Collins's 'Squad' struck, killing 14 suspected British intelligence officers in their Dublin homes. In the afternoon, British forces opened fire on a crowd at Dublin's Croke Park during a Gaelic football match between Dublin and Tipperary, killing 14. In the evening, Dick McKee, Peadar Clancy and Conor Clune were killed in controversial circumstances. On 28 November, 17 were killed and one left for dead when an ADRIC patrol was ambushed at Kilmichael, County Cork. Tom Barry later claimed that members of the patrol had feigned surrender, and that because of this the flying column did not take any prisoners; certainly, the engagement was unusually violent. It was followed by British reprisals and martial law, although policy remained trapped between the pressure to escalate and a reluctance to see the crisis as anything more than a police matter. Martial law was introduced, in a limited fashion, on 11

December for four counties – Cork, Kerry, Limerick and Tipperary. It was expanded to include Clare, Kilkenny, Waterford and Wexford in January 1921, but Dublin was not included.

However, British counterinsurgency in Ireland was not as clumsy as might be supposed. As William Sheehan has written, some historians still portray the British army 'as a lumbering giant around whom the pimpernels of the IRA ran rings' (Sheehan, *A Hard Local War*, p.16). The situation was a dynamic one in which both sides sought to innovate and respond to the changes of the other. For example, British intelligence improved during the conflict and was formidable by the time of the truce. Further, as Townshend has noted, the idea of an omniscient IRA is much exaggerated (Townshend, 'Irish Republican Army', p.329). British counter-guerrilla measures increasingly put the IRA on the defensive. The British launched sweeps that had much in common with those of the South African War. They put pressure on the IRA, but they also struggled to cope with the IRA's increasing use of the roadside bomb (the Improvised Explosive Device – IED – continues to pose a problem to regular forces today). The Crossbarry ambush (19 March 1921) was perhaps the closest thing to a battle during the conflict. For historians, it has proved to be a controversial episode, especially as so much has previously depended on Tom Barry's version of events. The traditional narrative was that the IRA, in a fighting retreat, held off a much larger British force than the one that was in fact present. Nonetheless, British losses were heavier, with ten killed to the IRA's six. Air power was used in several roles in Ireland, including reconnaissance and bombing. Indeed, the British commander in Ireland from 1920 to 1922, General Sir Nevil Macready, believed that air power would be decisive in the event of the truce (see below) breaking down. However, Chief of the Air Staff Hugh Trenchard was wary of the potential of negative press in Ireland, and the RAF was only used there in tightly controlled circumstances.

By 1921, the British faced a choice. As Macready put it, it was a case of 'all out or get out'. In the end, the former proved unpalatable. The

Lloyd George government was forced to pursue the latter course and negotiate a settlement, which ensured a face-saving exit. The British were keen to wind down their military commitments at a time of imperial overstretch. Diarmaid Ferriter has questioned whether the IRA was close to collapse, arguing it was too late for the British to redeem their political failures (Ferriter, *A Nation and Not a Rabble*, p.239). The IRA suffered heavy losses in a large raid on the Customs House on 25 May 1921; but their ability to mount the assault in the first place sapped British optimism that they were on the verge of defeat. Sinn Féin swept the board in the May 1921 Irish elections, winning all 124 seats in the south. Both sides agreed a truce, which came into effect on 11 July 1921; 624 members of the security forces, along with 752 IRA and civilians, had been killed in the conflict.

The Anglo-Irish Treaty was signed on 6 December, giving Ireland Dominion status. It was a triumph for Lloyd George, but proved divisive in Ireland. The ensuing Irish Civil War (1922–23), in which Michael Collins was killed, pitted pro-treaty forces against anti-treaty. However, the latter were outnumbered and outgunned (thanks partly to British support for the government). The war ended with the anti-treaty side downing arms on 24 May 1923. To defeat the anti-treaty forces, the government turned to repression, carrying out 77 executions (53 more than the British carried out during the War of Independence) and imprisoning some 11,480 more.

The Arab Revolt (1936–39)

On the eve of World War II, the British faced a challenging revolt in Mandatory Palestine. Clashes between Arab and Jewish populations had led to violence before. However, Jewish migration increased significantly following Hitler's rise to power in 1933, with the Jewish population more than doubling between 1931 and 1936. The Arab Revolt was a popular rising against both British Mandatory rule and Jewish immigration. The spark came on 15 April 1936, with an attack on a convoy on the Nablus–Tulkarm road in which two

Jewish passengers were killed. In the first phase of the revolt, Arab workers staged a general strike. This phase ended with a ceasefire in October, and the establishment of a Royal Commission, led by Lord Peel, which recommended that Palestine be partitioned. The second phase of the revolt began in 1937 with the rejection of the commission's conclusion and the assassination of the district commissioner of Galilee, Lewis Andrews, on 26 September. The zenith of the insurgency came in autumn 1938, when the British lost control of Jerusalem for five days in October. However, the conclusion of the Munich Agreement with Hitler at the end of September 1938 provided the opportunity to send reinforcements to Palestine. By the end of the year, the British had deployed more than 20,000 men to re-establish control. The revolt symbolically ended with the government's White Paper of May 1939. It was overtaken by events, since the outbreak of World War II diverted attention from Palestine. However, violence would resume with the Jewish insurgency of 1944–48, which led to British withdrawal and the establishment of the state of Israel (1948).

As Townshend has written, 'It was the very diffuseness of Arab resistance that rendered the struggle of 1936–39 more intractable than any other imperial crisis between the wars' (Townshend, 'The Defence of Palestine', p.918). Martial law was never declared in Palestine, but the army took de facto control in the second phase. Indeed, the Colonial Office replaced the High Commissioner, Sir Arthur Wauchope, with Sir Harold MacMichael in March 1938, which not only eased civil–military relations but also smoothed the path for the army to take over. As in the South African War, large-scale operations included sweeps, and the construction of a blockhouse and barbed-wire system (to seal the eastern border), although the latter did not prove as effective as that of 1899–1902. 'Destruction and vandalism,' Matthew Hughes has argued, 'became a systematic, systemic part of British counter-insurgency operations during the revolt, and justified by the legal measures in force at the time' (Hughes, 'The Banality of Brutality', p.320). In June 1936, in the most notable example of demolition, the British destroyed 15 per cent of the buildings in old Jaffa. Beyond such measures, there were 'unofficial' reprisals. As Hughes has written, the British 'used force across a spectrum: not so much minimum force as necessary force and, at times, excessive force', although punitive measures usually stopped short of atrocity (Hughes, 'From Law and Order to Pacification', p.18). However, there were two notable exceptions. At al-Bassa, in September 1938, the British killed 20 villagers after a mine had killed two men, with two more dying from their wounds. At Halhul in May 1939, 15 died after being left in a cage in the heat with insufficient water.

Perhaps the most famous development of the counterinsurgency campaign was the creation of the Special Night Squads (SNS). Tom Bowden called them 'the shock-troops of the British military response', although he also noted they were 'merely one arm of the massive constant pressure and harassment exerted upon the rebels' (Bowden, 'Arab Rebellion in Palestine', p.166). The activities and significance of the SNS have remained controversial, as has the career of their founder and leader, the charismatic Orde Wingate (1903–44). Simon Anglim, in his 2014 biography, situated Wingate's military thought and the SNS firmly in the continuum of established British imperial thought and practice. Indeed, in a recent article, Preston Jordan Lim argued that the SNS were no more brutal than the army as a whole. He contended that too much attention has been paid to this aspect of the SNS, and too little to their role in intelligence, 'showing the flag', and increasing understanding between the security forces and Jewish settlers. Hughes, on the other hand, argued that the SNS fought a 'dirty war', in which the army's basic tactics could be 'escalated and aggravated' by an unorthodox force. The army's unease with Wingate's 'off-the-grid' operations led to the SNS being closed down in autumn 1938 (Anglim, *Wingate*, p.28; Lim, 'The Prickly Thorn', pp.92–93; Hughes, 'Terror in Galilee', p.595).

The revolt's diffuseness might have been a strength, as we have seen, but historians have questioned whether it could have succeeded. Hughes has argued that the revolt was a 'bottom-up' insurgency, in which the lack of leadership, effective networks of resistance and a clear objective cost the rebels dear. On the other hand, historians have noted the success of British operations. Hughes has highlighted the effectiveness of the British pacification campaign, especially after the 'surge' in 1938, while according to Jacob Norris, 'it was military might that eventually led the British counterinsurgency to prevail' (Norris, 'Repression and Rebellion', p.35). By 1939, over 9,000 Arabs were being held in prisons and detention centres, and Hughes estimates that over 7,000 were killed during the revolt (Hughes, *Pacification of Palestine*, p.382).

Writing About Imperial Policing: Britain in the 1930s

As T. R. Moreman has noted, although attention to the subject was not systematic, by 1939, there was a good range of material available on small wars and imperial policing in Britain (Moreman, '"Small Wars" and "Imperial Policing"'). Prominent examples included the official 'Notes on Imperial Policing' (1934), Major-General Sir Charles W. Gwynn's *Imperial Policing* (published in 1934, with a second edition following in 1939) and H. J. Simson's *British Rule, and Rebellion* (1937). This material recognised, as the official manual noted, that the armed forces were 'called upon from time to time to carry out operations for the maintenance or restoration of internal peace' ('Notes on Imperial Policing', p.5). Indeed, this was not just throughout the empire, but also at home, as Britain experienced significant labour unrest in the 1920s and 1930s. A crucial event for British counterinsurgency was the Amritsar massacre, where on 13 April 1919, troops under the command of Brigadier-General Reginald Dyer had fired on a crowd which had gathered in the Jallianwala Bagh, killing 379 people (this was the official figure, and the real number is likely to have been somewhat higher). A major theme of the subsequent material available on imperial policing was that there was a need to 'nip trouble in the bud' but without undue severity. As the official 'Notes on Imperial Policing' suggested, 'The principle which has consistently governed the policy of His Majesty's

Government in directing the methods to be employed when military action in support of civil authority is required may be broadly stated as the use of minimum force necessary' (Ibid, p.41).

Gwynn, who had been commandant of the Staff College from 1926 to 1930, sought to capture the lessons of Britain's extensive experience in his *Imperial Policing*. The first two chapters of the book established key principles, with the rest of the book going on to examine a series of case studies. Like Callwell, Gwynn divided campaigns into three classes; and realised that the category of classic 'small war' had come to an end and that at the time of writing the use of the army to restore order (his second category) was of special importance (his third category was aid to the civil power). His book was about the consolidation of empire, rather than its expansion. It was this role which, he believed, created the major challenge. Gwynn noted the difficulties of hunting small bands of guerrillas, and understood that the population might have divided loyalties making the job of the counterinsurgent harder. Force could not be excessive but must be enough to demonstrate resolve.

He believed that recent history showed 'that the Army can be trusted to act with good sense and restraint', even though his first case study was Amritsar (Gwynn, *Imperial Policing*, p.2). For Gwynn, Dyer had failed to follow correct principles. In Egypt in 1919 and Palestine in 1929 (to give two examples), he argued that principles were largely adhered to. Ultimately, Gwynn was suggesting that exemplary violence would convince opponents, neutrals and loyalists alike of British determination and, thereby, would win the campaign. Gwynn chose to leave out Britain's experience in Ireland, saying only that it would be 'inadvisable' to include it (Ibid, p.8). Simson, on the other hand, did draw on the lessons of the Irish conflict. He coined the term 'sub-war' to describe insurgency, which he defined as 'an organised use of force, partly under arms, designed to get something by force against the will of the properly constituted government' (Simson, *British Rule, and Rebellion*, p.36). He argued that sub-war could not be met 'by the laws and punishments of ordinary times' (Ibid, p.96). To gain a quick decision, it was necessary to take the offensive, as in other forms of warfare. He called for systematic combing, area by area, in order to (re)establish control and for co-ordination all areas of the counterinsurgency – civil, police, legal and military – in order to ensure unity of purpose. Sub-war should be defeated before any 'yielding' (he chose this word deliberately) of concessions: 'It is better to win first and then give' (Ibid, pp.118–19). Simson's reflections on the need to study particular cases provide an interesting perspective on the gap between theory and practice; like 'the difference between reading and seeing a play', he suggested (Ibid, p.131). Simson saw British rule as positive, attempting to guide its empire to a state of free cooperation and, therefore, not 'imperialist'. However, in rejecting moderation and calling for prompt measures, his approach certainly justified exemplary violence.

Gwynn and Simson both saw the Arab Revolt as demonstrating how a government showing weakness could cede the initiative to rebels. Gwynn was critical in his 1939 edition, as was Simson, who tellingly described Palestine as 'an Ireland number two' (Ibid, p.168). He criticised what he saw as a reactive and conciliatory government policy and called for a greater sense of purpose and better coordination. A General Staff report, 'Military Lessons of the Arab Rebellion in Palestine, 1936' (1938), came to the same conclusion. In the long run, repressive measures saved lives because conciliation suggested weakness in the face of force. The 'weapon of martial law' was more merciful in the end because 'The bigger the stick the less likely is one to risk being struck by it' (p.32). It is clear that by 1939 ideas on the moral effect of exemplary force, especially when used against peoples whom British commentators saw in racial terms as less civilised, were still deeply engrained.

Conclusion

Although the idea of guerrilla warfare, the weak versus the strong, is as old as warfare itself, recognisable techniques of modern counterinsurgency emerged from the end of the 18th century. By 1939, a body of ideas on how to fight against irregular opponents had emerged in the West, thanks to the experience of fighting colonial warfare and the codification of principles by the likes of Callwell, Gwynn, Simson and Lyautey. National and other ideological movements that arose after World War II would pose even greater challenges to counterinsurgent forces.

The Rise of Communist Insurgency and Protracted People's War

On 7 and 8 November 1917, the Bolsheviks led by Vladimir Lenin seized power in Russia, toppling the Provisional Government led by Alexander Kerensky. The coup followed Lenin's model of an urban revolution launched by a professional cadre of communist revolutionaries: the vanguard. Key buildings like the Central Telegraph Office, Nikolaevskii Railway Station and the Winter Palace were captured. Although the takeover was relatively peaceful, the deep fractures created led to a five-year civil war from which the Bolsheviks eventually emerged victorious, establishing the Soviet Union in 1922. The Leninist vanguard coup remained one of the dominant approaches to insurgency until Mao's victory in China in 1949 demonstrated the effectiveness of his strategies.

The Chinese Civil War (1927–49) saw the rise of Mao Zedong, whose ideas of a 'protracted people's war' would shape the West's understanding of communist insurgency for much of the 20th century. Unlike the Russian approach that focused on cities, Mao argued for building popular political support among the rural peasantry. This would isolate the established authority over time and ultimately lead to its replacement with a communist state.

The strategy required insurgents to act justly towards the peasantry and to earn their support. The war would be won over three phases: the strategic defensive where the opponent's forces would be defeated through conventional and guerrilla operations would be followed by a strategic stalemate. During this time, the legitimacy of the government would be challenged through guerrilla operations and the development of rival political and social structures. The final

Mao Zedong's ideas of 'protracted people's war' shaped the West's understanding of communist insurgency.

phase, the strategic counter-offensive, would see the insurgents attack the enemy's centres of power to gain complete control.

After the success of Mao's Chinese Communist Party, scholars looked to understand the new strategies. They uncritically accepted claims of the few Western observers, like Edgar Snow, who had visited the communists in the 1930s, and a simple narrative of Mao's guerrilla victory emerged. In reality, Mao had won by skilfully exploiting nationalist weakness and division; he conscripted manpower, requisitioned supplies and ruthlessly suppressed opposition; militarily he used a combination of guerrilla tactics, siege warfare and regular armies. Despite later successful communist revolutions in Cuba (1953–59), Vietnam (1954–75) and Cambodia (1975) employing different strategies, Mao's ideas of winning a protracted war by operating amongst the people remained dominant even into the era of global insurgency.

CHAPTER 2

Counterinsurgency, 1945–2000

The dawn of the Cold War gave a powerful new impetus to insurgency and counterinsurgency. Nationalist, communist and anti-colonial movements could look to the USSR or the People's Republic of China for external support. Meanwhile, the Western powers tried to manage their withdrawal from empire while the United States attempted to halt the spread of communist regimes by propping up existing systems.

This chapter will examine two different experiences of counterinsurgency during this period. It will first look at the French counterinsurgency experience, which shows the complex relationship between theory and practice. It will consider *guerre révolutionnaire* (revolutionary war), a theory of warfare developed by the French. It will focus on two French authors in particular: Roger Trinquier and David Galula. Trinquier argued that the character of war had changed, and that counterinsurgency was a subset of what he called 'modern war'. Trinquier's writing was more influential at the time than Galula's, but the latter is considered here because his work was rediscovered in the 21st century by US counterinsurgency writers. *Guerre révolutionnaire* was the product of the French army's reading of Mao, but it was also a result of its painful experience of defeat in Indochina (1946–54) against the communist Viet Minh. This chapter will also examine France's Algerian War (1954–62) in depth, one of the largest (and most brutal) counterinsurgency campaigns of the modern era.

Second, this chapter will look at the US experience of counterinsurgency. The obvious focus here is the Vietnam War (1954–75). It is an important case study because it features so prominently in the history of counterinsurgency, as an example of a failed campaign. Traditional explanations for US defeat include the contention that the war was essentially unwinnable and should never have been fought at all, and that the US got the counterinsurgency part of the war badly wrong. However, recent scholarship has cast doubt on such arguments, suggesting that the US did counterinsurgency far better than the traditional view has accounted for, and that the US lost the war because of a complex mixture of factors: some beyond its control, and some which were the result of bad strategic choices.

France and *Guerre Révolutionnaire*

In developing the theory of *guerre révolutionnaire* (revolutionary war) French military theorists drew on several sources. First, they were aware of previous imperial experience, especially the legacy of Galliéni and Lyautey. However, the traditional methods of colonial warfare were deemed to be insufficient. The experience of war in Indochina (1946–54) seemed to bear this out, as the French succumbed to the Viet Minh's revolutionary war. Therefore, second, the theorists of *guerre révolutionnaire* sought to understand the lessons of the painful defeat in Indochina. Third, they studied Maoist theory. *Guerre révolutionnaire* owed much to the idea that contemporary events could be understood through the lens of a worldwide communist conspiracy. As Commandant Jacques Hogard wrote, it was 'the war of revolution for the conquest of the world. This war has become permanent, universal, and truly global' (Cradock and Smith, 'No Fixed Values', p.75). As such, the war, according to theorists of *guerre révolutionnaire*, was already happening, whether anyone in France liked it or not. Peter Paret noted in his 1964 study, *French Revolutionary Warfare*, that its strongest feature was its comprehension that the symbiotic relationship between the political and military elements of revolutionary movements constituted a source of power. As Hogard wrote, 'revolutionary warfare is very different from traditional conventional war. Widely dispersed from the outset, it gradually draws strength and resources from the enemy, seeking to capture not military or geographical objectives, but the population' (Paret, *French Revolutionary Warfare*, p.18.)

The result was that *guerre révolutionnaire* was seen, as Finch has noted, as a form of 'total war' (Finch, 'Total War of the Mind', pp.410-414). In order to defeat revolutionary insurgency, *guerre révolutionnaire* called for the same degree of political mobilisation on the counterinsurgent side. As Paret has written, 'In the eyes of the theorists of *guerre révolutionnaire*, the war in Algeria became part of a greater crusade for the spiritual and national future of France,' (Paret, *French Revolutionary Warfare*, p.28). However, the 'win at all costs' mentality that *guerre révolutionnaire* sought to foster meant that the ends justified the means. The French army would turn to the use of torture and other forms of brutality. As Paret has written, 'Officially they formed no part of the doctrine of *guerre révolutionnaire*, but they belonged to its reality', and it was, therefore, 'difficult to avoid the conclusion that the doctrine of *guerre révolutionnaire* contains a high potential of political explosiveness' (Ibid, pp.66, 120). Furthermore, given that *guerre révolutionnaire* presupposed global communist subversion, it would not help the French to understand the national, regional and local dynamics of their opponent in Algeria – the National Liberation Front (*Front de Libération Nationale* or FLN). A further problem was that, as we have seen with previous colonial conflicts, the wars in Indochina and Algeria were total for the Viet Minh and the FLN but were not for the French. This asymmetry is an important explanation for French defeat in both conflicts, just as it would be for the US defeat in the Vietnam War.

The Algerian War

In the centre of Algiers, there is a square named Place Maurice Audin. Formerly known as Place Maréchal Lyautey, it was renamed in 1963 in honour of Audin, an assistant professor at the University of Algiers, member of the Algerian Communist Party and supporter of the FLN, who was arrested during the 1957 Battle of Algiers. Audin was said to have disappeared until, on 13 September 2018, French President Emmanuel Macron admitted the French military authorities were directly responsible for his death. This historic occasion was the first time the French government had officially admitted the authorities had systematically employed torture during the Algerian War. Recognition of what happened in Algeria between 1954 and 1962 had been a long time coming. Indeed, it was only as recently as 1999 that the government recognised that a state of war had existed at all.

The Algerian War is surely the signature event in the demise of the French Empire. As Martin Thomas has written, 'The Algerian War was longer, bigger and nastier than anything in the British experience' (Thomas, *Fight or Flight*, p.315.) Some two million French troops were deployed in total, with a peak strength of 500,000, as well as thousands of other service personnel (on 1 January 1959, there were over 35,000 air-force personnel in Algeria), gendarmes and police. Between 250,000 and 300,000 are thought to have died, roughly the same percentage loss for Algeria as France suffered in World War I. Two factors were crucial in defining the character of the war. First, Algeria was part of metropolitan France. As we saw in Chapter 1, the French invaded Algeria in 1830. From 1848, Algiers, Oran and Constantine were organised as *départements* of France. Second, the presence of a large settler community – known as *colons* or *pieds noirs* – meant that Algeria itself was divided by race, class, and culture. By the end of World War II, there were some one million settlers and some nine million Algerians. By 1945, the French faced an increasingly prominent nationalist movement, and, as had happened elsewhere, World War II destabilised the basis of colonial rule. As Martin Evans has put it, the 'long hatreds' (Evans, *Algeria*, pp.19–48) produced by the original French invasion constituted one thread in the origins of the conflict, the emergence of modern Algerian nationalism another. A state of undeclared war could be said to have existed from 1945. At Sétif in May 1945, rioting in which 106 Europeans were killed was met with severe repression by French security forces, with an unknown number of Algerians massacred in response.

The FLN was established in 1954, with its military wing, the *Armée de Libération Nationale* (ALN). The war opened on All Saints Day (1 November) 1954, known as *Toussaint Rouge* (red All Saints Day), with multiple FLN attacks against police and military targets. The FLN issued a proclamation outlining their strategy:

> GOAL. National independence through: 1) restoration of the Algerian state, sovereign, democratic, and social, within the framework of the principles of Islam; 2) preservation of all fundamental freedoms, without distinction of race or religion.
>
> INTERNAL OBJECTIVES: 1) political house-cleaning through the destruction of the last vestiges of corruption and reformism, the causes of our present decadence.
>
> EXTERNAL OBJECTIVES: 1) internationalization of the Algerian problem; 2) pursuit of North African unity in its national Arabo-Islamic context; 3) assertion, through United Nations Charter, of our active sympathy towards all nations that may support our liberating action.
>
> MEANS OF STRUGGLE: by every means until the realisation of our goal … action abroad to make the Algerian problem a reality for the entire world … the struggle will be long, but the outcome is certain. (Horne, *A Savage War of Peace*, p.95)

As Evans has written, 'Guns alone gave the FLN the right to speak for the nation' (Evans, *Algeria*, p.117). On 12 November, Pierre Mendès France, the French Prime Minister, told the National Assembly that France would not give in:

> One does not compromise when it comes to defending the internal peace of the nation, the unity and the integrity of the Republic. The Algerian departments are part of the French Republic. They have been French for a long time, and they are irrevocably French... Mesdames, Messieurs, several deputies have made comparisons between French policy in Algeria and Tunisia. I declare that no parallel is more erroneous, that no comparison is falser, or more dangerous. Ici, c'est la France! [Here, it is France]. (Horne, *A Savage War of Peace*, p.98)

The years 1955–56 saw the widening and deepening of the war. In Algeria, the Philippeville massacre (20 August 1955), in which the FLN killed over 120 people, led to severe reprisals by French and settler forces, and a hardening of the French line. In February 1956, Guy Mollet became French Prime Minister. He sought a 'third way' but faced pressure from the settler population. Mollet initiated what would today be called a 'surge', flooding Algeria with extra troops. By July 1957, France had 450,000 men in Algeria. This meant calling up the reserve, and on 18 May 1956, a party of 21 reservists were killed in the Palestro gorge, which signified the war was now taking the lives of ordinary Frenchmen. Internationally, the Algerian right to self-determination was asserted at the Bandung Conference of non-aligned states in April 1955. The FLN held a crucial conference in the Soummam valley in August 1956, which reaffirmed the international strategy. The FLN would seek to make French military victory impossible, whilst isolating it politically. The international arena was, as Martin Alexander and J. F. V. Keiger have written, 'absolutely decisive for achievement of an independent Algeria' (Alexander and Keiger, 'France and the Algerian War', p.18). The Cold War context meant that the US feared Soviet subversion, and was keen to win over Algerian nationalist opinion without antagonising France. In October 1956, the arrest of one of the leaders of the FLN, Ahmed Ben Bella, backfired badly and encouraged Morocco and Tunisia to back the FLN'S effort. The French bombing of Sakiet in Tunisia on 8 February 1958 antagonised the Tunisian President, Habib Bourguiba. Alistair Horne has suggested that no event did more to internationalise the conflict (Horne, *A Savage War of Peace*, pp.249–250). Finally, the Suez Crisis (October–November

1956) had a profound impact on the Algerian War. In French eyes, the two conflicts were linked by the figure of Egyptian President, Gamal Abdel Nasser. The Anglo-French climbdown following landings along the Suez Canal was a humiliation, and for the French army, it was another step in its increasing disillusionment with the Fourth Republic. French paratroopers were redeployed from Suez to Algeria, and they would play a central role in what would become the most famous event of the war.

The battle of Algiers (1956–57) was immortalised by Gillo Pontecorvo's 1966 film of the same name. As Alexander and Keiger have written, the battle 'was notable for the ruthlessness shown by both sides. The gloves came off and the struggle in Algeria became a truly "dirty war" (*une sale guerre*)' (Alexander and Keiger, 'France and the Algerian War', p.9). On 7 January 1957, the resident minister, Robert Lacoste, handed over full powers to General Jacques Massu, commander of the 10th Parachute Division. The paratroopers moved into the Casbah in Algiers in a massive cordon and sweep operation. Massu's main object was to destroy the FLN's organisation, rather than capturing individuals or equipment. This goal was certainly achieved, but the use of torture was widespread, and one estimate is that over 3,000 extrajudicial killings took place. As Christopher Cradock and M. L. R. Smith argue, there was little in the way of winning hearts and minds here, beyond the use of terror (Cradock and Smith, 'No Fixed Values', pp.68, 102). However, the extent to which the battle of Algiers was the 'most graphic expression' of the doctrine of *guerre révolutionnaire* is debatable. Aside from the potential for extreme behaviour inherent in counter-revolutionary war, a range of other contingent factors influenced the army's actions, such as the effect of its previous experiences in Indochina, Algeria and during the Suez Crisis. In any event, the use of torture on captured suspects was politically disastrous. Leaking news about interrogation methods caused uproar, reflected in exposés such as French-Algerian journalist Henri Alleg's *La Question* (1958) and in the critical writings of intellectuals such as Albert Camus and Jean-Paul Sartre. As police chief Paul Teitgen said, 'Massu won the

Battle of Algiers; but that meant losing the war' (Horne, *A Savage War of Peace*, p.207).

In Algiers and elsewhere, the French instituted a system of *quadrillage*, in which areas were divided into a grid system, each grid being swept by patrols. This was a standard counterinsurgency technique, but it was inefficient, as the British had found in South Africa and Palestine. It required large numbers of troops who were not always able to pin down the hard-to-catch insurgent fighters. The army was, therefore, forced to undergo a difficult process of innovation and adaptation. One improvement was the construction of defensive barriers, which were policed by mobile patrols. The French began work on the most notable of these barriers, the Morice Line, in September 1957. This ran along the Algeria–Tunisia border and was designed to cut the FLN off from its external sources of support. The French established *Sections Administratives Spécialisées* (SAS) in May 1955 as part of their pacification effort. The SAS eventually numbered 5,000 personnel spread across 800 rural centres. They were expected to win 'hearts and minds' but also formed a central part of the military campaign (for example, by providing valuable intelligence). They were complemented by *Sections Administratives Urbaines* (SAU) in the cities. The *Cinquième Bureau* was responsible for psychological warfare, including propaganda and disinformation. Captain Paul-Alain Léger's operation in Algiers in 1957 was particularly effective, his network of 'turned' FLN breeding suspicion and confusion among FLN ranks.

The intensification of the war had a drastic effect on French politics. The events of the May 1958 crisis brought down the Fourth Republic – the Fifth Republic was born following a referendum on 28 September, and Charles de Gaulle became its first President in January 1959. In the meantime, de Gaulle visited Algiers on 4 June. '*Je vous ai compris*,' he told the crowd ('I understood you'). De Gaulle purged the army, removing General Raoul Salan from command and replacing him with General Maurice Challe (from December 1958 to April 1960). Challe was given the resources he needed – in

May 1959, he commanded 394,500 French troops. Significantly, the French also made increasing use of Algerian troops, the *harkis*, with some 58,000 in the field by the end of 1959. The 'Challe Plan' involved a series of large-scale military operations; the largest of which was Operation *Jumelles* (Binoculars), which opened in July 1959 and lasted eight months. Mass resettlement was also a feature. The army had moved 1,282,000 people by January 1960. The Challe Plan was what would today be called 'enemy-centric' counterinsurgency, and it produced significant operational successes. It is estimated that it destroyed some 40–50 per cent of the armed groups. However, it did not bring overall victory. Politically, de Gaulle's 'self-determination' speech on 16 September 1959 made it clear that there were three alternatives: secession of Algeria from France, integration (Algeria remaining part of France) and association (a third way, favoured by de Gaulle, in which Algeria would become independent but would retain a connection to the French Empire). De Gaulle's words ('*Je vous ai compris*') and actions (the Challe Plan) suggest, as Irwin Wall noted, that he desired to keep Algeria bound to France. However, his vision foundered without the cooperation of the FLN and the *colons*, and more favourable international opinion (Wall, 'De Gaulle', p.121).

Growing disquiet among hardliners erupted after Massu criticised government policy in an interview published on 18 January 1960. This 'Bombe Massu' led to his dismissal and was the pretext for an attempted settler insurrection that became known as the 'Week of Barricades'. De Gaulle held firm, giving a crucial address to the nation on 29 January, which marked the turning point of the crisis. He visited Algeria again in December, during which 'Algeria for Algerians' demonstrations suggested there was no alternative to the FLN. On 8 January 1961, France voted in favour of self-determination for Algeria. In response, hardliners established the *Organisation Armée Secrète* (OAS) to prevent independence. In April, Generals Challe, Salan, Jouhaud and Zeller, launched a military putsch. Once again, de Gaulle remained calm, giving another masterful performance in a speech on 23 April when he asked the people of

France to help him (*'aidez moi'*). The putsch collapsed, although the OAS's attacks continued, reaching their peak after the 1962 Évian Accords brought the war between the French government and the FLN to an end. The OAS killed over 2,000 people before they were finally defeated by French troops. Salan was captured in April. Algeria celebrated its independence in July and, during the course of the year, most of the settler population departed the country. The war remains a seminal event in Algerian history and has become a byword for brutality. As Martin Thomas has noted, the British were fighting colonial counterinsurgencies at the same time, but 'forced decolonisation did not significantly damage the fabric of civil-military relations in Britain. In the French case, it almost destroyed it' (Thomas, 'The British Government and the End of French Algeria', p.193).

Perhaps the most famous event of the Algerian War, the **battle of Algiers** (1956–57) saw French paratroopers under the command of General Jacques Massu move into the Casbah in Algiers in a massive cordon and sweep operation, which aimed to destroy the FLN's organisation. Thousands of arrests were made, but the security forces tortured and killed suspects; a fact which generated huge controversy at the time and which was only recently admitted by the French government. French conduct during the battle helped to ensure that the French would win militarily but lose politically. The events of the battle were depicted in Gillo Pontecorvo's 1966 film, *The Battle of Algiers*, which is now widely regarded as a masterpiece and a realistic depiction of urban insurgency.

French Counterinsurgency Theory: Trinquier and Galula

Roger Trinquier (1908–86) fought in Indochina and Algeria. He published his reflections in a short book called *La Guerre Moderne* (1961), translated into English as *Modern Warfare: A French View of Counterinsurgency* (1964). Trinquier viewed conventional war as 'traditional' war, which was now obsolete. For Trinquier, revolutionary war was *modern war*. From this observation, the rest of his analysis flowed. Trinquier argued that 'the *sine qua non* of victory in *modern warfare* is the unconditional support of a population'. The enemy was not a few armed bands, but 'an *armed clandestine organisation* whose essential role is to impose its will upon the population' (Trinquier, *Modern Warfare*, pp.8–9). He provided detailed advice on how this organisation might be destroyed. Since the population was the centre of the conflict, the people needed to be prepared and organised, social programmes were to provide them with what they required to maintain normal activities and a propaganda campaign needed to make it clear what they were fighting for. Guerrilla forces depended on popular support and on access to supplies; they were to be cut off from these and defeated by attrition. The key was in the proper deployment of resources. Trinquier believed that in Indochina and Algeria, the French had hesitated to take vital steps. He called for all necessary measures to be taken to win, just as in traditional warfare. This was the sort of 'total war' rhetoric that legitimised the 'means justify the ends' approach inherent in *guerre révolutionnaire*.

David Galula (1919–67) fought in World War II and later in China, Greece, Indochina and Algeria. While a fellow at the Center for International Affairs at Harvard he wrote *Counterinsurgency Warfare: Theory and Practice* (1964). In contrast to Trinquier, his work seems to have languished in relative obscurity, until its rediscovery during the counterinsurgency revival in the 2000s, when it became a seminal influence on the US manual FM 3-24. John Nagl, in the foreword to the 2006 edition, wrote that 'Galula's primacy of place in the canon of irregular warfare is secured by his lucid instructions on how counterinsurgency forces can protect and hence gain support of the populace, acquire information on the identity and location of insurgents, and thereby defeat the insurgency' (Galula, *Counterinsurgency Warfare*, p.vii). Galula argued that revolutionary war was exceptional, not just because it had 'its special rules, different from those of the conventional war, but also because most of the rules applicable to one side do not work for the other. In a fight between a fly and a lion, the fly cannot deliver a knockout blow and the lion cannot fly' (Ibid, p.xii). Mao, he suggested, had codified the rules of the revolutionary side; the principles of counter-revolutionary warfare needed to be found elsewhere. Galula, therefore, sought to be the anti-Mao. The basic theory was that the counterinsurgent enjoyed the advantages when it came to 'tangible' assets, whereas the insurgent had the upper hand in 'intangibles', in the form of a cause. Thus, the insurgent could not go toe to toe with the counterinsurgent and, therefore, needed to shift the fight to new ground – namely, the population. The most difficult challenge for the counterinsurgent was developing a plausible counter-narrative or cause of their own. As Galula wrote, 'Whereas in conventional war, either side can initiate the conflict, only one – the insurgent – can initiate a revolutionary war, for counterinsurgency is only an effect of insurgency. Furthermore, counterinsurgency cannot be defined except by reference to its cause' (Ibid, p.1).

Aside from a cause, the other necessity for a successful insurgency was 'a police and administrative weakness in the counterinsurgent camp'. An advantageous geographical environment and external support were also helpful (the latter potentially essential). Because counterinsurgency required its own principles, Galula suggested the following: the support of the population was equally necessary for both sides; neutrals within the population needed to be won over to the government's side; support was conditional and relied on the strength of the counterinsurgent side; and intensity of effort was essential. The destruction of the insurgency required a step-by-step strategy in which the counterinsurgent would take on the insurgent on their own ground, in the battle for the population. As such, the political had primacy over the military in counterinsurgency: "A revolutionary war is 20 per cent military action and 80 per cent political". The armed forces would need to adapt to carry out a range of different tasks, but these principles could be taught. The essence of revolutionary war, Galula argued, was to 'Build (or rebuild) a political machine from the population upward' (Ibid, pp.63, 67, 95).

Trinquier saw traditional warfare as outdated and emphasised the challenges of what he called 'modern warfare', and in so doing, he was overemphasising the extent to which the character of war had really changed. Galula saw counterinsurgency as inherently more complex than conventional war. This is a trap that others have fallen into since, not least some of Galula's admirers in the 21st-century US Army.

The United States and the Vietnam War

Defeat in Vietnam was a watershed moment for the United States. It divided politics, society and the military, and left a global super-power soul-searching over what had gone so wrong. The orthodox view is that the US should not have fought the war in Vietnam and that it was unwinnable. However, key US policymakers were motivated by the feeling that there was a need to take a stand in Vietnam in the interests of American security and international order. There was a widespread and genuine belief in the 'domino theory'; China's fall to communism seemed to confirm it. If the Vietnamese 'domino' fell it seemed inevitable that other countries would follow. The perceived lesson of the Munich Agreement with Hitler in 1938 was that appeasement did not pay. Of course, these assumptions are open to question.

It is also debatable whether the war was indeed unwinnable. To answer this question, attention should be focused on the strategic options available to the US. In Vietnam, it fought against a commu-nist insurgency, backed by the regular forces of communist North Vietnam. Ho Chi Minh and his subordinates were fighting to unify Vietnam under a communist regime, not a nationalist one. The war also had an important international dimension. Communist forces received vital aid from the Soviet Union and China. US policymakers feared that both could be drawn more directly into the conflict if it escalated: these fears were understandable. In any case, as Jeffrey Record has written, the US 'underestimated the patience, tenacity and military capacity of the Vietnamese communists while at the same time inflating its own power to prevail over what was, after all, an impoverished, preindustrial state' (Record, *The Wrong War*, p.29). Fundamentally, the US failed to recognise the disparity in commitment between the two sides: what was a limited war for the US was far more total a conflict for their Vietnamese communist opponents. As Record has written:

> The United States abandoned its cause in Indochina because it was strategically, politically, fiscally, and morally exhausted. Never prepared (nor should it have been) to make anything remotely approaching the proportional sacrifices in blood and treasure in Indochina that its communist enemy was willing to – and did – make, and being a democracy in which official policy fundamentally hostile to the electorate's wishes could not be indefinitely pursued, the United States withdrew from Vietnam because it had no other choice. The critical domino at stake in the Vietnam War was American public opinion, to which Hanoi seemingly paid longer and more profitable attention than did the White House.

A major issue in the debate over strategic choices was the question of whether the US had focused too much on counterinsurgency or not enough. The classic statement of the argument that the Americans had overemphasised counterinsurgency was Colonel Harry G. Summers's book *On Strategy: A Critical Analysis of the Vietnam War* (1982). Summers noted that: 'On the battlefield itself, the Army was unbeatable. In engagement after engagement the forces of the Viet Cong and of the North Vietnamese Army were thrown back with terrible losses. Yet, in the end, it was North Vietnam, not the United States, that emerged victorious. How could we have succeeded so well, yet failed so miserably?' (p.1). Summers argued that more 'conventional' fighting, not less, was the key to victory. He argued that the 'national will' had not been mobilised, that strategy making had been dominated by civilian analysts, that fear of China and the Soviet Union had paralysed strategic thinking, and that counterinsurgency 'became not so much the Army's doctrine as the Army's dogma, and ... stultified military strategic thinking for the next decade' (Ibid, p.73). Summers argued that 'South Vietnam faced not only internal insurgency but also outside aggression' and, therefore, counterinsurgency doctrine, although it had much to offer, only provided part of the answer (Ibid, p.77). He argued that the US had entered the war on the strategic defensive:

> instead of orienting on North Vietnam – the source of war – we turned our attention to the symptom – the guerrilla war in the south. Our new 'strategy' of counterinsurgency blinded us to the fact that the guerrilla war was tactical and not strategic. It was a kind of economy of force operation on the part of North Vietnam to buy time and to wear down superior US military forces. (Ibid, p.88).

On the crucial home front, Summers argued that 'Our inability to explain in clear and understandable language what we were about in Vietnam undercut American support for the war' (Ibid, p.161).

The contrary view, that the US had focused too much on destroying the enemy's armed forces and not enough on pacification, was most clearly put in Andrew Krepinevich's book, *The Army and Vietnam* (1986). Krepinevich, paraphrasing words used by Omar Bradley to describe the escalation of the Korean War (1950–53) to include fighting China, referred to Vietnam as 'the wrong war – at the wrong place, at the wrong time, with the wrong army' (p.4). For Krepinevich, the army failed in large part because it was more interested in fighting the war it had prepared for, in other words a firepower-heavy conventional war. The 'other war', the pacification campaign, lacked the kind of centralised direction across the range of activities that were necessary for a successful counterinsurgency.

The Geneva Accords (1954) were not a peace treaty but merely provided a ceasefire. The US had successfully defended the Republic of Korea against the Democratic People's Republic in the Korean War, and it still maintained troops there. The US, therefore, supported South Vietnam. In 1954, head of state and former Emperor Bao Dai appointed Ngo Dinh Diem (1901–63) as Prime Minister. The following year, Diem held a referendum that allowed people to choose between himself and Bao Dai as leader of South Vietnam. His victory with over 90 per cent of the vote was highly dubious but it allowed him to depose Bao Dai and declare the formation of the Republic of Vietnam (RVN), with himself as President. The deadline for elections to decide Vietnam's future came and went, and the partition of the country became an established fact. However, the existence of the RVN was never recognised by North Vietnam, nor did the North ever see itself as a separate state. The war was part of an ongoing communist revolution (which would culminate with reunification of the country in 1975 under the rule of Hanoi, in the North), and to that end, communist subversion increased in the South. To provide the movement with greater coherence, the Hanoi government declared the establishment of the National Liberation Front (NLF) in December 1960. The Southern insurgents soon became more famously known as the Viet Cong (VC). The US erred in seeing the NLF as merely a tool of the North, missing the chance to isolate some of the disparate elements in the South from Hanoi's influence.

If the US wanted to ensure the existence of South Vietnam, it would have to work with the RVN's leadership. Stanley Karnow's judgement of Diem is typical: he 'filled a vacuum, but despite his record of integrity, he lacked the dimensions of a national leader' (Karnow, *Vietnam*, p.229). Diem's rule would be blighted by corruption and repression, and he would eventually be overthrown by a coup, with US connivance, on 1 November 1963. His overthrow produced instability that only ended when Nguyen Van Thieu (1932–2001) became President in 1967; he remained in office until the republic fell to North Vietnam in 1975.

The weakness of South Vietnam as a client state is advanced frequently as a major cause of US defeat. Jeffrey Record has even suggested that the South's defeat in 1975 would have happened in 1965 had it not been for the Americanisation of the war. 'The United States,' he argues, 'could not have picked a more intractable enemy and a feebler ally than it did in Indochina' (Record, *The*

Wrong War, p.173). However, it is easy to be overly critical of Diem, who offered an alternative to communism. It is open to question whether the US would have been better off backing Diem. Indeed, Mark Moyar probably went the furthest of the revisionists, arguing that Diem was an 'effective leader' whose war effort was succeeding when he was overthrown (Moyar, *Triumph Forsaken*, p.xiv). Diem not only asserted his country's independence but also, in Michael Kort's words, was 'doing the United States a favour by keeping it out of the war. By sponsoring Diem's overthrow, Washington opened the door to the Americanization of the Vietnam War' (Kort, *The Vietnam War Reexamined*, p.116).

The Americanization of the war took place in stages. Initially, Americans were sent as 'advisors'. The US established Military Assistance Command, Vietnam (MACV) on 8 February 1962, under the command of General Paul D. Harkins. Harkins was succeeded in June 1964 by General William C. Westmoreland. From 1965 onwards, US troop commitment to Vietnam ramped up significantly, peaking at 543,000 in spring 1969. On 28 July 1965, President Lyndon B. Johnson gave a press conference at which he said:

> This is a different kind of war. There are no marching armies or solemn declarations. Some citizens of South Vietnam at times, with understandable grievances, have joined in the attack on their own government. But we must not let this mask the central fact that this is really war. It is guided by North Vietnam and it is spurred by Communist China. Its goal is to conquer the South, to defeat American power, and to extend the Asiatic dominion of communism …. I have asked the Commanding General, General Westmoreland, what more he needs to meet this mounting aggression. He has told me. We will meet his needs …. We will stand in Vietnam. (President Johnson's News Conference, 28 July 1965)

American strategy following the establishment of MACV, and especially following the appointment of Westmoreland, is often characterised as being conventional, attritional, firepower heavy and focused on 'body count'. Depictions of the 'American way of war' see this approach as being deeply engrained. As Michael Herr put it in his famous *Dispatches* (1977), 'Search and Destroy, more a gestalt than a tactic, brought up alive and steaming from the Command psyche' (p.58). One of the central explanations for US defeat is that the army, once it became clear it was fighting the 'wrong' war, failed to learn and was, therefore, defeated. Prominent here is John Nagl, who compared the US approach unfavourably to that of the British during the Malayan Emergency (1948–60) in his 2002 book *Learning to Eat Soup with a Knife*. However, here too historians have offered differing views. The army devoted plenty of attention to counterinsurgency before Vietnam. For example, Mao's writings were influential in America as they had been elsewhere. The US Army's doctrinal manual FM 31–16 *Counterguerrilla Operations* recognised that counterinsurgency usually required policing operations (focusing on population control and security), separation of the guerrillas from the population and destruction of guerrilla units, military assistance in a programme of civil improvement and denial of sponsoring power support (if applicable). Gregory A. Daddis has argued, in his article 'Eating Soup with a Spoon', that 'Far from being culturally wedded to conventional concepts, many serving officers willingly pondered, debated, and learned about how best to adjust their approach to war in an unconventional setting' (p.240). The error is to judge everything the US did in Vietnam as a failure, simply because they lost.

One of the better-known aspects of the American approach was the 'body count'. In the absence of a clear front line, measuring enemy killed seemed to offer a way of determining progress. However, there were several problems with 'body count'. At the strategic level, it said little about US progress in the pacification campaign or about the success of the RVN and its army – the ARVN. At the operational and tactical levels, it was difficult to establish reliable figures for enemy killed. The demand for body counts led to inflated claims, helped to reinforce American reliance on firepower and, in the worst cases, could encourage indiscriminate killings in order to boost figures, along the lines of 'If it's dead and Vietnamese, it's VC.' In fact, a major problem for the Americans was that they had too much information. 'Statistics were, admittedly, an imperfect gauge of progress,' wrote Westmoreland in his memoir, *A Soldier Reports* (1976), 'yet in the absence of conventional front lines, how else to measure it?' (p.273). As Daddis has written, 'numbers whetted an appetite for more numbers' (Daddis, 'The Problem of Metrics', p.85). For example, the new Hamlet Evaluation System (HES) established in 1967 generated an average of 90,000 pages of reports per month, and the army was producing a weight of 14,000 pounds of reports per day. 'That the army never could determine if it was winning or losing,' Daddis notes, 'goes far in explaining the final outcome of the war in Vietnam' (Ibid, p.98).

The controversy over Westmoreland's performance has always been a major feature of the historiography. Even within the last few years, works have appeared at opposite ends of the spectrum. For example, the title of Lewis Sorley's biography, *Westmoreland: The General Who Lost Vietnam* (2011), says it all. Sorley was highly critical of what he saw as wrong-headed strategy, but most of his ire was reserved for Westmoreland's attempts to shape the historical record. He contended that Westmoreland was a conventionalist who failed to appreciate the problems with the body count. At Ia Drang in November 1965, the Americans inflicted casualties of 12 to one on their opponents, but the American people did not care about the 12; they cared about the one. At the opposite end of the spectrum, Dale Andrade also made his argument explicit in the title of his 2008 article 'Westmoreland was Right: Learning the Wrong Lessons from the Vietnam War'. Gregory Daddis's recent book, *Westmoreland's War*, published in 2014, also revises the thesis that the US lost in Vietnam because of bad leadership and an incorrect strategy. Daddis argues that such explanations are overly reductive. Indeed, they ignore many of the peculiar circumstances of the Vietnam War. The US faced both an insurgency *and* a conventional threat, in the form of the North Vietnamese Army. As Westmoreland wrote in *A Soldier Reports*, 'Ignore the big units and you courted disaster. Failure to go after them in at least comparable strength invited defeat' (p.99). The communists also possessed secure lines of retreat into neighbouring Laos and Cambodia. The ARVN was designed as a conventional force, but as Westmoreland noted in his memoirs, there was little alternative: 'There is nothing to prevent larger units from being broken down into smaller, more mobile forces when the occasion demands; it is considerably more difficult suddenly to transform small, disconnected units into large cohesive ones' (Ibid, p.58). The fact that South Vietnam was ultimately overrun by a conventional invasion justified the decision to set up the ARVN in this way.

Indeed, it was Westmoreland who implemented many of the war's pacification programmes and presided over reform in the US counterinsurgency effort. He was aware of the theory of insurgency: he kept a copy of Mao beside his bed, along with the works of Bernard Fall (a keen observer of the French experience in the war against the Viet Minh), although by his own admission he was 'usually too tired in late evening to give the books more than occasional attention' (Ibid, pp.277–78). He believed that the communists were following the Maoist framework of insurgency. He was certainly very conscious that the Viet Minh had decisively defeated the French at Dien Bien Phu in spring 1954: for example, his memoirs refer to the comparison between Dien Bien Phu and the US battle at Khe Sanh (1968). An important reform, supported by Westmoreland, was 'A Program for the Pacification and Long-Term Development of South Vietnam' (PROVN), produced in March 1966. PROVN recommended that the US pursue a tried-and-tested counterinsurgency method – the 'oil spot' strategy. Andrew J. Birtle, in a 2008 article on PROVN, argued that Westmoreland understood the importance of pacification and the shortcomings of large-scale sweeps, and that there was less disagreement between Westmoreland and PROVN's authors than many commentators have suggested. Indeed, PROVN's most important objective was the defeat of the enemy's main forces. In 1967, the Americans established the Civil Operations and Rural Development Support (CORDS) programme. President Johnson appointed Robert W. Komer to act as Westmoreland's deputy for pacification and to head CORDS. At its peak, CORDS employed some 5,500 officials. However, as Daddis has written, 'CORDS, like so many of the US Army's programmes, never came to grips with the underlying problems of the war inside South Vietnam', such as the gap between the government and people of the RVN (Daddis, 'Eating Soup with a Spoon', p.253). Violence against civilians also helped to derail pacification. Most notorious is the My Lai massacre of March 1968, although focusing on this one event can obscure the extent to which such violence was produced by widespread racism, overuse of firepower and deliberate policies such as body count.

Large-scale spectaculars, rather than slow-burning pacification programmes, attracted the world's attention. Operation *Rolling Thunder* began on 2 March 1965. Originally due to last only eight weeks, it ended up lasting over three years. By the end of the war, American, South Vietnamese and allied aircraft had dropped some eight million tons of bombs: most of it on the South or in Laos and Cambodia against communist supply lines. The traditional argument is that *Rolling Thunder* failed because guerrillas, backed by an agrarian North Vietnam, were immune to a bombing campaign. However, revisionists have focused on the restricted, on-again off-again nature of the bombing, which ultimately did not coerce the North Vietnamese leadership.

Large 'search and destroy' operations were also prominent. In the Ia Drang Valley in November 1965, the Americans inflicted heavy losses on the People's Army of Vietnam (PAVN), but also suffered 500 casualties of their own. Lieutenant-Colonel (later Lieutenant-General) Harold G. Moore wrote in his famous account of the battle, *We Were Soldiers Once ... And Young* (1992), that 'This was America's war now, and America had never lost a war' (p.398). Operation *Masher/White Wing*, in early 1966, was launched in the coastal province of Binh Dinh; this was followed by Operations *Thayer*, *Irving*, and *Thayer II* in the autumn and winter. In January 1967, Westmoreland launched *Cedar Falls*, the largest American ground operation of the war, which aimed to eliminate a VC stronghold called the 'Iron Triangle'. At the end of February 1967, Operation *Junction City*, the largest airborne operation of the war, sought to destroy the Central Office for South Vietnam (COSVN); the reputed headquarters of the VC (the so-called 'bamboo Pentagon', which never existed in the centralised way the Americans believed it did). However, operational successes did not lead to strategic victory. The communists were able to administer a severe shock to the Americans with the Tet Offensive of 1968. Launched on 31 January to coincide with Tet, the lunar new year, communist forces attacked in more than 100 cities and towns. Most famous were the attacks on Saigon, especially on the US embassy, and on Hué, where the Marines and South Vietnamese forces fought a bitter battle to wrest back control of the city and its citadel. Communist losses were heavy, including many of the VC's best men. The offensive was far too broad in scope (both geographically and chronologically, with further offensives in May and August) and allowed the Americans to play to their strengths (for example, in firepower). However, Tet has gone down in history as a political triumph for the communists. It showed that the war was far from won, as images from Vietnam played on TV screens across the world. On 31 March, Johnson told the country he would not seek another term as President. General Creighton Abrams, who had been appointed Westmoreland's deputy in May 1967 and was being lined up to replace him, became commander of MACV in June 1968. As Andrade recognises, we can accept that ultimately Westmoreland failed because he lost the war. However, perhaps the key point here is that Westmoreland lacked the resources or opportunity to handle both the conventional and the guerrilla threats. As Daddis has written:

> Westmoreland developed a comprehensive strategy for Vietnam, one not confined to simple attrition of enemy forces. The implementation of that strategy, however, failed to resolve the underlying issues of the war and, in the process, highlighted the limits of American military power abroad during the Cold War era. (Daddis, *Westmoreland's War*, p.xx)

Marines riding on top of an M-48 tank cover their ears as the 90mm gun fires during a road sweep southwest of Phu Bai in April 1968. (532483: US Marine Corps)

Abrams would preside over a different kind of war. Richard Nixon won the 1968 election and 'Nixon's war' would include as one of its central planks a policy of 'Vietnamization', in which the South Vietnamese would assume greater responsibility for the war effort and would be equipped to defend themselves. US troops would be progressively withdrawn. American strength peaked at 543,000 in spring 1969, but thereafter, Abrams had to make do with what he had. However, as Birtle and others have noted, Abrams also relied on firepower and large-scale actions. For example, one of the most famous battles of the war was for Hill 937, or 'Hamburger Hill' as it is now more famously known, in May 1969. 'Rather than representing antithetical concepts,' Birtle wrote, 'Westmoreland's and Abrams's approaches to the conflict were cut of the same cloth, and we should not allow minor differences to mask this fundamental truth' (Birtle, 'PROVN, Westmoreland, and the Historians', pp.1246–47). The difference was that Abrams benefited from the military victory of Tet, while Nixon's extension of the war into Cambodia (in 1970) and Laos (in 1971) were a setback to the PAVN and a boost to the ARVN. Sorley's *A Better War* (1999) contrasted what he saw as the successes of the Abrams years with what had gone before, arguing that the improved conduct of the war meant that the US achieved a 'lost victory' in Vietnam. The PAVN staged a 'regular' invasion of the South in the Easter Offensive of 1972, which was successfully stopped by the South's armed forces with US air support (Operation *Linebacker* – a large-scale bombing campaign). Indeed, it is tempting to see the war as having been won at this point; the internal security situation in the South had improved, and the ARVN fought well to blunt the Easter Offensive. Continued resistance by the RVN required an open-ended US commitment. This was not impossible in principle: the US maintained permanent forces in West Germany and South Korea at this time. After the signing of the Paris Peace Accords in January 1973, American support for the South dwindled. The North launched another major offensive in 1975, and Saigon fell on 30 April. The communists had achieved their overall aim of reunifying the country under their rule, while the US had failed to maintain the existence of an independent RVN.

The US Army's response to Vietnam was to bury it as a painful experience not to be repeated. A powerful idea took hold that the USA should fight 'no more Vietnams', indeed should avoid fighting another counterinsurgency campaign at all. The army turned to what it was good at, fighting conventional warfare against a peer opponent, and focused on planning for a war against the Soviet Union, from which would emerge the concept of AirLand Battle. With the collapse of the Soviet Union, AirLand Battle was instead put into practice against Iraq following its invasion of Kuwait in 1990. The lightning success of the ground war in February 1991 seemed to show that the US Army had conquered its Vietnam demons. However, the aftermath of the US invasions of Afghanistan (2001) and Iraq (2003) demonstrated that counterinsurgency could not be ignored.

Conclusion

It is often argued that the Vietnam War represents an example of how not to do counterinsurgency. However, this traditional narrative has come under fire in recent scholarship on the war and with good reason. The US put more into their counterinsurgency effort than is often realised. They failed because of a host of intractable problems. These included the need to focus on the conventional threat offered by the North Vietnamese, weaknesses in the South Vietnamese polity and the fact that, ultimately, there was a significant asymmetry between the US conduct of what was to them a limited conflict, and the communist prosecution of what was for them a far more 'total' war.

The French war in Algeria and the US experience in Vietnam are two of the most famous counterinsurgency campaigns of the 20th century, but both showed the gap between theory and practice, and both showed that simplistic narratives will not do. The causes of French and US defeat were complex, and they remain hotly debated today. Algeria and Vietnam have provided plenty of evidence for subsequent generations of counterinsurgency writers, but their 'lessons' proved to be far from straightforward, and the interpretation of these lessons depended on the agendas of those writing.

Moreover, Algeria and Vietnam were only two of the many counterinsurgency campaigns fought around the world after World War II. The Algerian War is an example of a European power fighting a counterinsurgency at the end of the age of European empires, and Algeria successfully won its independence. During the same period, Portugal fought the Angolan War of Independence (1961–74) against various insurgent groups (the eventual victor following a subsequent civil war being the People's Movement for the Liberation of Angola – the MPLA). It also fought against the Mozambique Liberation Front (*Frente de Libertação de Moçambique*, FRELIMO) between 1964 and 1975. The results were a military coup which overthrew the Portuguese Estado Novo in 1974, and independence for Angola and Mozambique in 1975. Britain also fought several wars of decolonisation against insurgencies. Its extensive experience helped to foster the idea that the British had a special approach to, and talent for, counterinsurgency; a subject that will be explored in the next chapter.

CHAPTER 3

A British Way in Counterinsurgency?
1945–2000

Just as during the periods 1815–1914 and 1918–39, the British army has fought numerous counterinsurgency campaigns since 1945. Until 1970, these were mostly wars of empire. The idea that there was a 'British way in counterinsurgency' developed as a result of observations of Britain's practical experience, and of the codification of principles based on this experience in theoretical writing. Many counterinsurgency experts have portrayed the British campaign during the Malayan Emergency (1948–60) as a model. The British soldier-scholar Robert Thompson (1916–92), in his book *Defeating Communist Insurgency* (1966), developed a set of principles based on Malaya and the ongoing war in Vietnam, emphasising the rule of law, civil–military coordination and the need to prioritise countering political subversion rather than winning military victory (Thompson, *Defeating Communist Insurgency*, pp.50–58). 'Winning the hearts and minds of the people' became a handy catchphrase, which seemed to encapsulate the key reason for British success in Malaya. Many subsequent authors followed this line. For example, Thomas Mockaitis, in his *British Counterinsurgency, 1919–60* (1990) and *British Counterinsurgency in the Post-Imperial Era* (1995) argued that the British way was defined by three broad principles: minimum force, close civil-military cooperation and a decentralised, flexible, small-unit approach (Mockaitis, *British Counterinsurgency,* pp.13–14).

As the British manual, *Imperial Policing and Duties in Aid of the Civil Power* (1949) noted, 'The establishment of mutual confidence between the civil, the police and the military authorities at all levels is of the first importance.' It also stressed that 'There is … one principle that must be observed in all types of action taken by the troops, no more force shall be applied than the situation demands' (p.5).

During the boom in interest in counterinsurgency that began after the invasions of Afghanistan and Iraq, the 'British way' became a renewed focus of interest. One of the foremost examples was the theorist-practitioner John A. Nagl, author of the widely cited *Learning to Eat Soup with a Knife: Counterinsurgency Lessons from Malaya and Vietnam* (2002), co-creator of the US counterinsurgency doctrine FM 3-24 (2006) and a veteran of the Iraq War. The core of Nagl's argument was that:

> The better performance of the British army in learning and implementing a successful counterinsurgency doctrine in Malaya (as compared to the American army's failure to learn and implement successful counterinsurgency doctrine in Vietnam) is best explained by the differing organizational cultures of the two armies; in short, that the British army was a learning institution and the American army was not. (Nagl, *Learning to Eat Soup with a Knife*, p.xxii)

The counterinsurgency boom was shortly followed by a wave of revisionism that began to debunk many of the established narratives, among which was that of the 'British way'. First, several works questioned the idea that the British were particularly good at counterinsurgency. For example, Andrew Mumford's *The Counterinsurgency Myth* (2012) argued that Britain's quantity of counterinsurgency experience was too easily taken to mean commensurate quality in approach, whereas, in fact, the British were 'slow learners and slow strategic burners in the realm of counterinsurgency warfare' (p.1). Frank Ledwidge's *Losing Small Wars* (2011) contended that many (including himself) bought into the idea of a 'British way', leading to disillusionment when experience in Iraq revealed major failings at the operational level (p.6). Moreover, the circumstances of Afghanistan and Iraq, where Britain would conduct counterinsurgency campaigns in 'host' countries, would be entirely different to, for example, Malaya, where there was a British colonial administration already in place. Finally, Hew Strachan suggested that 'the campaigns in the 1950s and 1960s were actually predicated on the presumption of Britain's military defeat: Britain was getting out' (Strachan, 'British Counter-Insurgency from Malaya to Iraq', p.10).

There was also increasing doubt as to whether the British approach really emphasised minimum force in practice. 'When we speak about "hearts and minds,"' Hew Strachan noted, 'we are not talking about being nice to the natives, but about giving them the firm smack of government. "Hearts and minds" denoted authority, not appeasement. Of course, political and social reform might accompany firm government' (Ibid, p.8). Books such as David French's *The British Way in Counterinsurgency, 1945–1967* (2011) and Huw Bennett's *Fighting the Mau Mau: the British Army and Counterinsurgency in the Kenya Emergency* (2013) revised the 'minimum force' narrative and returned exemplary violence to the story. French argued that in practice British approaches were determined by perceptions of their enemies, which involved marginalising and criminalising them rather than accepting legitimate grievances. A lack of resources meant that in practice, 'winning hearts and minds' was either undesirable or too expensive. The concept of 'minimum force' was highly malleable (who decides what is the minimum necessary?), and operating within the law was no guarantee of minimum force, given that the authorities were willing and able to expand and use their powers (especially by emergency regulations) when it suited them. French argues that the British army was less of a successful learning organisation than Nagl and others believed. Finally, changes in British domestic and international politics had a significant impact on what the British could and could not do. Although not covered in French's book, the British deployment to Northern Ireland in Operation *Banner* (1969–2007) perhaps illustrated this point better than any other; the British army was forced to operate under the spotlight of both domestic and international opinion.

This chapter will, therefore, explore the case studies of the emergencies in Malaya (1948–60), Kenya (1952–60), and Cyprus (1955–59), as well as the Troubles in Northern Ireland. It will also examine the writings of Robert Thompson and Frank Kitson (1926–), two prominent theorist-practitioners of counterinsurgency. A major theme will be continuity and change. Techniques such as sweeps and resettlement were iterations of methods used during the South African War, but it is also clear that different contexts affected what the British could and could not do. Moreover, Britain's extensive experience of small wars was no guarantee that lessons would be learned and 'passed on'. The idea of a British 'retreat from empire' that was more orderly and less violent than the decolonisation processes of, for example, the French and Portuguese Empires, is a questionable one. As David Anderson has written, 'It would be foolish to contest between them to find the worst, the one with the most atrocities, or the highest number of assassinations, mutilations or defilements: there is nothing to be gained from a league table that measures the order of barbarity' (Anderson, *Histories of the Hanged*, p.6). It was not clear in 1945 that the empire would have almost completely disappeared within a few decades, and decolonisation was a complex process in which policymakers sought to manage a range of crises across the globe, often with the use of force. The British generally enjoyed the advantage of already having an administration in place with which they could fight colonial insurgencies, but in Malaya, they were able to use the promise of independence as a significant 'carrot' to go with the coercive 'stick'.

Instead of seeing 'hearts and minds' and 'butcher and bolt' as an either/or, we should see violence as a spectrum: levels of force used varied depending on time and space. Moreover, as Daniel Branch has noted, non-military 'hearts and minds' methods did not make counterinsurgency non-violent or any less punitive (Branch, 'Footprints in the Sand', p.17). If the Malayan Emergency really was the pinnacle of the British approach, it is necessary to consider that a very different kind of campaign was going on in Kenya at the same time. Anderson has suggested that 'there is something compellingly distinctive about the institutional bureaucratization of war in Kenya that sets it apart from other examples' (Anderson, *Histories of the Hanged,* p.6). We also need to bear in mind the Cold War context that made Malaya different. Of the campaigns considered here, only Malaya was fought against communist opponents, and even here, the British tended to overestimate the role of the hidden hand of Soviet or Chinese influence. Although it is convenient to refer to the 'British' (as this chapter will do) when discussing colonial counterinsurgency, locally recruited allies were a vital component and stood behind what was usually a 'thin white line' British element. Finally, the search for general principles, of which Thompson and Kitson are such recognised exponents, runs up against the problem that each counterinsurgency has its own characteristics, which need to be understood. What worked in one time and place does not necessarily work in another.

The Malayan Emergency (1948–60)

Of all the British counterinsurgency campaigns, it is the Malayan Emergency that is most often seen as a providing a model for success and a counterpoint to US failure in Vietnam. Far from this being merely a case of British writers trumpeting their own success story, American authors have also been prominent here. John J. McCuen heralded Britain's important contribution in his 1966 book *The Art of Counter-Revolutionary War: The Strategy of Counter-Insurgency,* while more recently, Nagl argued that the British succeeded in Malaya because its army was a superior learning organisation to that of the US.

The Malayan Communist Party (MCP) was founded in 1930. Its leader during the Emergency, Chin Peng (1924–2013), rose to prominence during World War II, when Malaya was occupied by the Japanese. The MCP cooperated with British forces during the period of the occupation, but the war rocked the foundations of colonial rule in South-East Asia, and the British found it difficult to reassert control after the Japanese surrender in 1945. The MCP planned to commence their insurgency in September 1948, but the British declared a state of emergency following the murders of three European planters on 16 June. Opposing the government was the MCP's Malayan National Liberation Army (MNLA), as it was known from 1949, supported by a civilian organisation, the *Min Yuen* (Masses Organisation). Crucially, 90 per cent of the MNLA was Chinese (there were two million Chinese in Malaya, compared with over five million Malays).

The initial British response was uncertain. The effectiveness of British administration left much to be desired, and the High Commissioner, Sir Edward Gent, had underestimated the nature of the threat. Gent returned to London, where he was killed in a mid-air collision over Northwood, and Sir Henry Gurney was appointed to succeed him in September 1948. To start with, the British largely focused on counter-terror operations. The sweeps conducted by the security forces were very much in keeping with the responses the British had employed in the South African War. Moreover, they put the insurgency under pressure, preventing the establishment of communist base areas and breaking up larger insurgent forces. However, the violence of the counter-terror phase led to controversy. Emergency Regulation 17 (D) permitted detention and repatriation, and thousands of 'squatters' (Chinese agricultural smallholders) were deported to China. By December 1951, as Loo Chow Chin has shown in his investigation of this subject, some 12,140 had been removed from Malaya. However, the repatriation policy was deeply flawed. There were logistical challenges involved in moving large numbers, the victory of the Communist Party of China in the Civil War in 1949 closed off China as a destination and the policy was, of course, open to serious criticism on humanitarian grounds (most obviously, Malayan-born Chinese were not actually from China) (Loo Chow Chin, 'The Repatriation of the Chinese', pp.363–392). At Batang Kali, on 12 December 1948, 24 men were killed by an army patrol. It was claimed at the time the men were shot while trying to escape, but evidence has emerged since to suggest they were massacred. The question of the extent to which such violence was condoned, or how typical it was, is difficult to answer. For example, Anthony Short has argued that Batang Kali stands out precisely because it is exceptional (Short, 'Batang Kali', p.346). In any case, more positive steps would need to be taken in order to bring the insurgency to an end.

Lieutenant-General Sir Harold Briggs was appointed Director of Operations in April 1950. He implemented the 'Briggs Plan'. The security forces would aim to dominate the populated areas of the country, break up the organisation of the *Min Yuen*, isolate the insurgents from their supplies and force them to fight on British terms as a result. The most significant aspect of the Briggs Plan was the resettlement of 500,000 squatters into what would become known as the 'New Villages'. These would allow the British to separate the guerrilla forces from the people. It was also believed that improving the conditions in which the squatters lived would increase their adherence to the state. That the Briggs Plan put the MCP under pressure can be noted from the fact that the insurgents stepped up their attacks in 1951. The MNLA peaked in size that year, as did the level of violence, but this was matched by the growing effectiveness of the security forces.

The increase in insurgent activity in 1951 did have one notable consequence. On 6 October 1951, insurgents attacked a convoy carrying Gurney, who was killed in what for the British was the lowest ebb of the counterinsurgency campaign. A month later, Briggs departed Malaya, suffering from ill health. Things looked bleak, although they were just as bad on the other side. Chin Peng issued his 'October 1951 Directive', in which he announced a change of tactics. The directive recognised that the insurgents were losing civilian support and operations would now focus on attacking the security forces. This was an admission that the insurgents' strategy was not working.

What would the British do next? 'We must have a plan. Secondly, we must have a man. When we have a plan and a man, we shall succeed: not otherwise.' So wrote Field Marshal Bernard Montgomery to the Secretary of State for the Colonies, Oliver Lyttelton, of the situation that faced the British in Malaya in December 1951 (Nolan, *Military Leadership and Counterinsurgency*, p.81). 'The man' chosen for the job was General Sir Gerald Templer, who arrived in Malaya on 7 February 1952 to take command of the British counterinsurgency effort. Following the assassination of Gurney and the departure of Briggs, the British took the opportunity to combine civilian and military authority in one post. Templer served as supremo from 1952 to 1954. He undoubtedly brought great energy to the role, overseeing improvements to the intelligence machinery and the police. New manuals were introduced, such as the army's *The Conduct of Anti-terrorist Operations in Malaya* (ATOM) in 1952, which collated experience and ideas about best practice across a whole range of areas, from intelligence, to patrolling and ambush, to the use of dogs. Training centres were established, such as the Federation Police Training College (1953) and Jungle Warfare School (1953). In making these improvements, Templer relied on some talented subordinates, such as his Director of Intelligence, John P. Morton, and his police chief, Colonel Arthur Young. Indeed, improvements in the British intelligence machinery were vital to the success of the Malayan campaign.

Templer's biographer, John Cloake, highlights above all his role as a coordinator of this activity. Templer paid special attention to the importance of winning 'the hearts and minds of the people': 'The shooting side of this business is only 25 per cent of the trouble and the other 75 per cent lies in getting the people of this country behind us', he wrote in November 1952 (Dixon, 'Hearts and Minds?', p.362). Templer paid special attention to the provision of land and sustenance in the New Villages, and to the creation of community spirit. However, he was happy to employ plenty of 'stick' to go with the 'carrot'. One of his first actions was to impose a collective punishment on the village of Tanjong Malim in the form of a 22-hour curfew. Although controversial, the curfew proved reasonably effective in allowing the gathering of intelligence on support for the communists in the area, leading to the arrest of some 40 suspects. Templer's dynamism also proved useful in ensuring complacency did not set in: 'I'll shoot the bastard who says this Emergency is over,' he famously told the *New York Herald Tribune* in April 1953 (Cloake, *Templer*, p.261).

Authors such as Cloake, John A. Nagl and Victoria Nolan have given Templer most of the credit for turning things around in Malaya. However, writers such as Karl Hack have suggested that the crucial period of the Emergency was 1950-52, although Templer was a 'brilliant optimiser of a changing campaign' (Hack, 'Everyone Lived in Fear', pp. 675, 693). Moreover, it is worth bearing in mind that Templer enjoyed a unique combination of powers. No British soldier since Cromwell had enjoyed such untrammelled civil and military authority. This certainly allowed Templer to get things done. Indeed, Briggs had not been entirely satisfied with the powers he had enjoyed. It seems best to conclude that there was no dramatic turning point, rather a series of processes which saw the initiative pass from the MCP to the security forces – and stay there. In 1953, Templer declared the first 'white' (insurgent-free) areas and by April 1954, 800,000 people were living in areas in which Emergency restrictions had been removed. Templer also understood the need for a common citizenship, and 1.1 million Chinese were enfranchised in September 1952 (along with some 2.7 million Malays and 220,000 Indians).

Templer departed on 31 May 1954, and the roles of High Commissioner and military commander were once again divided up. Sir Donald MacGillivray took over as High Commissioner and Lieutenant-General Sir Geoffrey Bourne became Director of Operations. One of the achievements of MacGillivray's tenure was the agreement to hold elections to the Federal Legislative Council. These took place in 1955, producing a majority for the Triple Alliance of Malay, Chinese and Indian parties. Tunku Abdul Rahman (1903–90) became the first Chief Minister. An amnesty was offered to Chin Peng, but he refused and the offer was withdrawn after the collapse of peace talks at Baling in December 1955. As Kumar Ramakrishna has shown, the idea that the period following Templer's departure only required 'mopping up' operations oversimplifies the picture, especially given that the MCP fighters who were left were the 'hardcore' who had refused to surrender previously. The British were increasingly effective at 'bribing the Reds to give up', with rewards for information and liberal surrender terms combining with the political and military eclipse of the MCP. The British granted independence to Malaya, which became a sovereign state on 31 August 1957, with the Tunku as its first premier. Independence (*Merdeka*) was followed by an amnesty (September) and a firm statement that there would be no more Baling-style talks. As Ramakrishna has shown, the communists were increasingly showing signs of war weariness; and with independence lending the government at Kuala Lumpur greater credibility, push and pull factors worked together to produce mass surrenders of insurgents in 1958 (Ramakrishna, 'Bribing the Reds to Give Up'; p.334).

The Emergency was officially declared over on 31 July 1960. Although the British had conceded independence, their longer-term interest was assured: namely, the existence of a friendly power which would help ensure the maintenance of British strategic interests in the Far East. The final toll of casualties was nonetheless high. A review of the Emergency produced by the Director of Operations after independence stated that the security forces had suffered 4,341 casualties and the insurgent losses were calculated at 9,158. Civilian casualties were given as 4,651 (French, *The British Way*, p.133).

As Karl Hack has argued, population and spatial control, as reflected in the New Villages, was the defining feature of British counterinsurgency in Malaya. The campaign blended coercion and 'hearts and minds', with the balance shifting between them (Hack, 'Everyone Lived in Fear', p.677). Indeed, Templer later referred to 'winning hearts and minds' as 'that nauseating phrase I think I invented' (Dixon, 'Hearts and Minds?', p.363).

The British benefited from a range of factors that were particular to Malaya. First, the fact that Malaya was a part of the British Empire meant that a structure of governance already existed, no matter how battered by the searing experience of World War II. It also meant that the British could choose their moment to play their trump card, the promise of independence, which effectively undercut the MCP. Second, the MCP never gained the support of the majority of the population. Its appeal remained limited to the Chinese population and it was never embraced by the Malays. This had much to do with the rubber boom of the early 1950s, which boosted the Malayan economy, as well as the promise of independence. The MCP also received little outside help. Even geography conspired against the MCP. Malaya was surrounded on three sides by sea and had only one land border, with Thailand to the north. Chin Peng himself crossed into Thailand in 1953, remaining in exile for the rest of his life. There were few places for the insurgents to go other than the jungles of the Malayan interior. Here, they could be defeated by British patrols and the use of air power. When looking at the success of the counterinsurgency in Malaya, it should be remembered that the unique circumstances which allowed the British to overcome the insurgents would not be available in other contexts.

Sir Gerald Templer (1898–1979) was commissioned into the army in 1916, serving in both World Wars. He arrived in Malaya in February 1952 and combined the roles of High Commissioner and Director of Operations from 1952 until 1954. Some argue his role was crucial in the defeat of the communist insurgency, while others suggest he simply continued a process already begun. Templer would serve as Chief of the Imperial General Staff (CIGS) from 1955 to 1958, and he was awarded his Field Marshal's baton in 1956.

Emergency in Kenya (1952–60)

In 2006, five Kenyans – Ndiku Mutua, Paulo Nzili, Wambugu Nyingi, Jane Muthoni Mara and Susan Ngondi – began civil proceedings against the UK government, claiming damages for mistreatment at British hands between 1954 and 1959. In 2011, Mr Justice

McCombe found that that the claimants had the right to sue the UK government. In June 2013, the then Foreign Secretary, William Hague, announced that the government had agreed 'payment of a settlement sum in respect of 5,228 claimants, as well as a gross costs sum, to the total value of £19.9 million'. Hague told the House of Commons:

> I would like to make clear now and for the first time, on behalf of Her Majesty's Government, that we understand the pain and grievance felt by those who were involved in the events of the Emergency in Kenya. The British Government recognises that Kenyans were subject to torture and other forms of ill treatment at the hands of the colonial administration. The British government sincerely regrets that these abuses took place, and that they marred Kenya's progress towards independence. (Statement to Parliament on Settlement of Mau Mau Claims, 6 June 2013)

However, in 2018, Mr Justice Stewart determined in the first test case in the group litigation of *Kimathi and Others* v *The Foreign and Commonwealth Office*, in which over 40,000 brought claims for damages, that the passage of time meant that there could not be a fair trial of the core allegations.

The Foreign and Commonwealth Office also admitted the existence of some 8,800 files that had been transferred to London by the colonial authorities ahead of independence, including documents from Kenya. In 2011, it was announced that these would be sent to the National Archives in London, and the process of release to the general public began the following year. The court case and the discovery of the 'migrated archives' showed that there was still much more to say about the nature of British counterinsurgency and the Kenya Emergency. The works of David Anderson, Caroline Elkins and Huw Bennett (all of whom were expert witnesses in the court case) have added much to our understanding of this controversial episode in British imperial history.

The nature of the British campaign in Kenya presents a challenge to the traditional narrative of a 'British way'. As Daniel Branch has written, '"Minimum force" hardly seems an appropriate label for the violence of the counterinsurgency in Kenya' (Branch, 'Footprints in the Sand', p.22). John Lonsdale referred to the campaign as 'the horror story of Britain's empire in the 1950s' (Lonsdale, 'Constructing Mau Mau', p.239). David Anderson described it as 'a story of atrocity and excess on both sides, a dirty war from which no one emerged with much pride, and certainly no glory' (Anderson, *Histories of the Hanged*, p.2). Indeed, the Kenya Emergency bears greater comparison to France's Algerian War than the 'British way' narrative allows.

On the eve of the Emergency, the European settler population was around 40,000. It continued to increase during the Emergency, reaching 61,000 by 1960. The settlers dominated the country but formed a minority of the population; there were over five million Africans living in Kenya at the start of the 1950s. Several factors led to violence, but perhaps none was as important as the land question. Loss of land became the number one grievance among the Kikuyu people from the 1930s, and Mau Mau emerged as a radical, militant Kikuyu movement. The origins of the term 'Mau Mau' are unclear. One explanation is that it was a distortion of the word *muma*, meaning oath. Widespread ritualised oath-taking began in the 1940s, and oathing and initiation ceremonies became a central focus of settler fears. The government introduced a counter-oathing programme, although this was not particularly successful.

In September 1952, Sir Evelyn Baring became Governor, replacing Sir Philip Mitchell. The assassination of one of the government's key supporters, Chief Waruhiu (who was heavily involved in the government's counter-oathing campaign), on 7 October 1952 gave Baring the pretext he needed to request a state of emergency. Huw Bennett has divided the conflict into four periods: an initial period of drift, a change in leadership with the arrival of General Sir George Erskine, Operation *Anvil* and a final surrender phase (Bennett, *Fighting the Mau Mau*, pp.11–12). The first of these began with Baring's declaration of the Emergency on 20 October 1952, and the counterinsurgency campaign went immediately into action. In Operation *Jock Scott*, security forces arrested 150 members of the Kenya African Union (KAU), including leader Jomo Kenyatta.

Within a few months of the declaration of a state of emergency, various significant events took place that set the tone for what was to follow. Kenyatta was put on trial in December and imprisoned. On 24 January 1953, Kenya was rocked by the news of the murders of a settler family, the Ruck family, by their servants. Such killings led to settler pressure on the government to take harsher measures, although Africans were more likely to be the victims of Mau Mau violence than Europeans. An event that historians often see as a crucial turning point is the Lari Massacre of 26 March 1953. The Mau Mau attacked the families of local chiefs and prominent Home Guard. In return, the Home Guard staged an even bloodier revenge attack. In total, some 400 were killed. Lari was important because it helped to consolidate the fault lines within Kikuyu society between Mau Mau, moderates and loyalists, and it led directly to a change of leadership on the counterinsurgency side.

The arrival of General Erskine in June 1953, replacing Brigadier Hinde as commander of forces in Kenya, marked the beginning of Bennett's second phase of counterinsurgency operations. Erskine commanded during the critical years of 1953–55, in which he imposed greater control and a clearer sense of direction. 'Mau Mau is not like a town riot which can be brought under control by a show of force,' he wrote to the CIGS, Field Marshal Sir John Harding on 15 August 1953. 'It is very deep.' (TNA CO 822/442) Therefore, it needed a long-term policy. In terms of the energy he injected into the campaign, he was not unlike Templer, although he did not enjoy the same powers. He was responsible only for military operations, although he carried the order from Churchill giving him the authority to assume greater powers in his glasses case and felt that the mere threat was enough. Erskine did not like Kenya and saw little hope for it. However, he also noted that there was no question of the government breaking down altogether. Bennett has noted that the settlers, the Kenyan administration, police and army all agreed on broad questions of policy and received the backing of the British government, which prioritised the defeat of the Mau Mau (Bennett, *Fighting the Mau Mau*, p.59).

The third phase began with the launch of Operation *Anvil* in April 1954. The Kenyan capital, Nairobi, was central to Mau Mau's logistics and a major source of recruits. *Anvil* showed that large 'cordon and sweep' operations could be very effective: it involved some 20,000 men, including British troops, a battalion of the King's African Rifles, police and Home Guard. By 9 May, over 23,000 people had been arrested. *Anvil* was, as Bennett has pointed out, a major turning point, and a defeat from which the insurgency never truly recovered because of Nairobi's importance as a logistical and manpower base (Ibid, p.24). The final phase of the campaign involved 'mopping up' of the remaining Mau Mau forces. Although the Emergency was not declared over until January 1960, militarily speaking the campaign was won by the end of 1956. The capture of Waruhiu Itote, 'General China' as he was known, in January 1954 was a major coup for the security forces. He agreed to cooperate with the British in exchange for having his death sentence commuted. The wounding and capture of one of the most important insurgent leaders, Dedan Kimathi, on 20 October 1956, was a notable victory that symbolised the end of effective resistance.

The counterinsurgency in Kenya, far from being based on 'minimum force', was characterised by coercion and brutality. Nonetheless, clearly the British expected higher standards of themselves. Excessive violence in pursuit of military necessity was seen as 'something the Germans did'. As Bennett put it, 'Erskine's major battle in 1953 was within the Army, not with the Mau Mau, to change the organization's culture … towards what he thought the traditional British method' (Bennett, 'The British Army and Controlling Barbarization During the Kenya Emergency', in Kassimeris (ed.), *Warrior's Dishonour*, p.71). He was particularly exasperated by the activities of Captain Griffiths of the King's African Rifles. Griffiths was court-martialled for murder but was found not guilty on a technicality, although he was convicted of a lesser charge in March 1954. A Court of Inquiry headed by Lieutenant-General Sir Kenneth McLean was established to investigate the army's conduct. On 26 January 1954, Anthony Head, the Secretary of State for War, reported to the House of

Commons that 'the troops in Kenya have shown a high sense of responsibility and application to duty. There do not appear to be any grounds for accusing them of indiscriminate shooting, irresponsible conduct or inhuman practices.' Cases of misconduct in the King's African Rifles were being investigated because 'our intention ... is for a clean-up, not a cover-up.' He concluded that, beyond these cases:

> nothing is disclosed which should in any way shake the confidence of the House in the high standard of behaviour of the British Army. As a result of reading the report and visiting Kenya, I am convinced that the British Army, under difficult and arduous circumstances, has shown that measure of restraint backed by good discipline which this country has traditionally expected. (Kenya (Report of Inquiry), 26 January 1954, Hansard, vol. 522, col. 1611)

In the aftermath of the Griffiths case, Erskine insisted that the army maintain its standards. 'I will not tolerate breaches of discipline leading to unfair treatment of anybody,' he wrote in a message for distribution to officers of the army, police and security forces in June 1953 (TNA WO 32/21721). However, the McLean Court of Inquiry did not consider events prior to Erskine's arrival and, therefore, did not provide a general overview. Moreover, the intentions of those at the top did not necessarily translate into realities on the ground.

One of the major explanations for the brutality of the campaign in Kenya was that it was as much a civil war as a counterinsurgency campaign. Branch has highlighted the importance of the emergence of a loyalist constituency in dealing a fatal blow to Mau Mau. As often happens in wartime, the fault lines were not necessarily drawn beforehand. Escalating violence forced people to take sides. 'Few factors solidified support for loyalism,' Branch has written, 'more than being the victim, or proximal to a victim, of Mau Mau's violence, regardless of past political allegiance or social standing' (Branch, *Defeating Mau Mau, Creating Kenya*, p.100). The conflict between the Home Guard and the insurgents was a bitter one, as events like the Lari Massacre demonstrate. The counterinsurgents employed repressive measures. Anderson's 'hanged' were the 1,090 sent to the gallows during the Emergency. As he notes, at no other time in the history of British imperialism was state execution used on such a scale (Anderson, *Histories of the Hanged*, pp.6–7). The most notable of these men was Dedan Kimathi, hanged in February 1957. Detention was used on a massive scale. Anderson estimated that some 150,000 were held in detention camps during the Emergency, with 70,000 the peak figure. Caroline Elkins, in her Pulitzer Prize winner *Britain's Gulag* (2005), estimated even more – 160,000–320,000 – although the latter has been criticised for being a considerable overestimate. As in Malaya, villagisation was used as a means of population control. If the numbers moved to the New Villages are included, some 1.5 million people in total were coerced – nearly the entire Kikuyu population. Kikuyu were 'screened'; a process Elkins examined in detail in *Britain's Gulag*. Detainees were colour coded according to how committed to Mau Mau they were deemed to be (with black being the level reserved for the most recalcitrant), and then processed through a 'pipeline' system. The euphemistic term 'screening' covered a range of interrogation methods, including beatings and torture. Some reviewers criticised Elkins for drawing comparisons to Stalin's gulags (as in the title of her book) and Nazi concentration camps, but her book played an important role in drawing attention to the cruelty of the Kenyan camps.

Bernard Porter, in a 2005 review of Anderson's and Elkins's books, asked of the counterinsurgency campaign: 'How did they get away with it?' In fact, the nature of Britain's 'dirty war' in Kenya was no secret: 'What is astonishing about Kenya's dirty war,' Anderson wrote, 'is not that it remained secret at the time but that it was so well known and so thoroughly documented' (Anderson, *Histories of the Hanged*, p.309). There were whistle-blowers: Eileen Fletcher produced an exposé of conditions at Kamiti camp, *The Truth About Kenya* (1956), in much the same way that Emily Hobhouse had done in the South African War. Barbara Castle, Labour MP for Blackburn, was a prominent critic of British policy and methods. Nevertheless, there was no outcry until the storm broke in 1959. On 24 February, the House of Commons debated a motion 'to institute an independent inquiry into the conditions and administration of prisons and detention camps in Kenya; and also to review the prolonged detention of men against whom no charges have been made' (Prisons and Detention Camps, Kenya, 24 February 1959, Hansard, vol. 600, col. 1019). Those who spoke against the motion focused on the brutality of Mau Mau, the process of rehabilitation and confidence in the government of Kenya and the prison service. Julian Amery, Under-Secretary of State for the Colonies, referred to 'the view that there were certain hard core elements [of Mau Mau] who, unless they became rehabilitated, could not safely be released', which prompted the striking interjection from Harry Hynd, MP for Accrington, 'That is what Hitler said' (Ibid, vol. 600, col. 1064). The House divided 288–232 against, but events would ensure that the issue would not go away. At Hola camp, 11 detainees were beaten to death in the 'Hola Massacre' of 4 March 1959. News of this event sparked a furore. On 27 July 1959, Hola was debated in the Commons in a dramatic session that lasted deep into the night. Mau Mau brutality was again a theme, with John Peel, MP for Leicester South East, referring to those who had taken the Mau Mau oath as 'sub-human'. It was gone midnight when Barbara Castle stood up to deliver a fiery speech. She asked:

> If in any prison in Britain twelve men had been beaten to death, would anyone on the benches opposite have said, 'Keep a sense of perspective about this, in view of the fine record of Prison Administration'? Of course not .... Quite instinctively, sincerely and genuinely, without even being aware of it, hon. Members opposite do not believe that an African life is as important as a white man's life. (Hola Camp, Kenya (Report), 27 July 1959, Hansard, vol. 610, col. 220, 231)

She concluded by suggesting that the Secretary of State for the Colonies, Alan Lennox-Boyd, stood in the dock as much as anyone else. Enoch Powell, who later became infamous for his 1968 'Rivers of Blood' speech, provided the most memorable attack: 'We cannot say,' he told the House, '"We will have African standards in Africa, Asian standards in Asia and perhaps British standards here at home." We have not that

choice to make. We must be consistent with ourselves everywhere ....
We cannot, we dare not, in Africa of all places, fall below our own
highest standards in the acceptance of responsibility' (Ibid, col. 237).
Here perhaps was the clearest demonstration of the gap between the
'British way' in theory and the reality of a camp in Kenya.

Historians have noted the significance of Hola, which made it
impossible for British rule to continue. As Elkins put it, 'The British
had won a long, costly, and bloody battle against Mau Mau, only
to lose the war for Kenya' (Elkins, *Britain's Gulag*, p.353). Indeed,
changes in key personnel represented something of a new broom.
Patrick Muir Renison was appointed Governor to replace Baring,
and Alan Lennox-Boyd was replaced by Iain Macleod at the Colonial
Office following an increased Conservative majority in the general
election in October. Macleod was determined to smooth the path to
decolonisation. The state of emergency was lifted in January 1960,
and Kenya became independent on 12 December 1963. Kenyatta
became the country's first Prime Minister (and first President when
it became a republic a year later, which he remained until his death
in 1978). During the Kenyatta years, and those of his successor
Daniel arap Moi, Mau Mau was essentially buried. Only recently
has Kenya begun to come to terms with its past; the recent court
cases and Hague's 2013 speech to the House of Commons suggest
Britain too has only just started the same process.

Emergency in Cyprus (1955–59)

The Cyprus Emergency makes for an interesting case study because it
took place contemporaneously to the latter stages of the emergencies
in Malaya and Kenya, but also because it took place in Europe, and
the counterinsurgency campaign was conducted against Europeans.
The British fought against EOKA (*Ethniki Organosis Kypriou
Agoniston*/National Organization of Cypriot Struggle), which sought
enosis – union with Greece. Led by George Grivas (1898–1974), a
retired colonel in the Greek army, EOKA provides a useful example

of an insurgency that was hard to beat because it 'swam' in the sea of a sympathetic population.

The Ottoman Empire ceded the right to administer Cyprus to Britain in June 1878. As a result of World War I, Britain claimed sovereignty, and Cyprus became a Crown Colony after the Treaty of Lausanne (1923). By the mid-1950s, nearly four-fifths of the island's population was Greek. The most significant minority were the Turks, who comprised 17 per cent. David French, whose book *Fighting EOKA* (2015) is the best study of the conflict, observed that *enosis* 'was more than a political programme. It was a cultural ideal that for many Greek Cypriots defined who they were' (p.23). The Orthodox Church played a central role. Michael Mouskos (1913–77), who became Archbishop Makarios III in 1950, proved to be an extremely effective politician. Makarios and Grivas represented the political and military wings of the *enosis* cause. The struggle for *enosis* would be conducted on multiple fronts: on Cyprus, in Greece (where much of the population was sympathetic to the Greek Cypriot cause), on the British home front, in Turkey (in its role as a regional player and protector of the Turkish Cypriot minority) and in the wider international community (especially at the United Nations and in the battle for support from the USA). The British counterinsurgency effort would, therefore, need to encompass all these areas.

EOKA's insurgency began on the night of 31 March/1 April 1955. Initially, it waged a sabotage campaign. EOKA was not well placed to mount a continuous campaign, nor were the British ready to respond. The campaign, therefore, began slowly for both sides. EOKA was not proscribed until September, but the conflict escalated that autumn. The Governor, Sir Robert Armitage, was blamed for being unprepared (in much the same way that Gent and Mitchell had been in Malaya and Kenya) and replaced by Field Marshal Sir John Harding. Harding came with clear ideas about what needed to be done, identifying four areas: rooting out terrorists, bringing the communists under control, demonstrating through propaganda the benefits of British rule and developing the economy and social services of the island.

For their part, EOKA intensified operations by launching Operation *Forward to Victory* on 9 October 1955. This featured a combination of rioting, bombings, sabotage, attacks on soldiers and police, and raids. Harding was given permission to declare a state of emergency, which he did on 26 November. Talks with Makarios broke down, and the archbishop was arrested on 9 March 1956 and deported to the Seychelles. Harding relied heavily on the army, with the garrison reaching 22,500 in June and 31,000 by the end of the year. He launched several large-scale operations, including the unfortunately named *Lucky Alphonse* in June, during which 21 soldiers died in a forest fire. This operation nearly captured Grivas, and during Operation *Whiskey Mac* in February–March 1957, Grivas's number two, Gregoris Afxentiou, was cornered and killed. Harding's operations put EOKA under serious pressure, and Grivas was compelled to call a truce in spring 1957 in order to regroup.

However, the outlook was not altogether rosy for the British. In the campaign for hearts and minds, the counterinsurgency faced an uphill struggle. As French put it, 'The single most important reason why the British lost that struggle was that the security forces were never able to lift the burden of EOKA intimidation from the necks of the Greek Cypriot community' (Ibid, p.158). EOKA was able to rely on willing support, but it was also able to coerce those who were less willing. Indeed, EOKA killed more Greek Cypriots than it did British soldiers. The state of the police was a major area of concern. As Andrew R. Novo has noted, the Cypriot police struggled. Greek Cypriots either sympathised with the insurgents or were successfully intimidated by them. The recruitment of more Turkish Cypriots to fill the ranks merely sharpened intercommunal tensions (Novo, 'Friend or Foe', pp.414–431). To use Mao's analogy, the British were not able to separate the fish from the water in Cyprus. The villagisation programmes employed in Malaya and Kenya were too expensive in time, money and manpower, but perhaps more importantly, they were not possible against Europeans and with the eyes of the world watching. As a result of these problems, the British, therefore, struggled to win the intelligence war. Harding's reforms improved the intelligence apparatus and enough information was gathered on EOKA that Grivas was nearly captured more than once. However, EOKA managed to achieve deeper penetration of the police than the British managed to do with EOKA, which allowed them to intimidate or kill informants and gain real-time information, especially on forthcoming security operations. EOKA was also able to wage an effective propaganda campaign, which spread news of British misbehaviour in order to ensure they would struggle to achieve popular support. The killing of Catherine Cutliffe, the wife of a British sergeant, in Famagusta (3 October 1958), one of the more famous events of the emergency, was criminal, but the angry British reaction provided EOKA with just what they were looking for. French has concluded that 'The security forces never behaved as badly as EOKA propaganda suggested they did …. But the security forces on Cyprus committed more misdemeanours than sanitized versions of the British campaign have suggested …. The insurgents had good reason to exaggerate misbehaviour by the security forces, and they did so with gusto' (French, *Fighting EOKA*, pp.235–36).

Following the debacle of the Suez Crisis, Prime Minister Anthony Eden resigned in January 1957, and Harold Macmillan formed a government. The release of Makarios was intended to open the way for negotiations. Harding was succeeded by Sir Hugh Foot as Governor on 3 December, but his arrival coincided with serious intercommunal violence. The Turks now had their own paramilitary organisation, *Türk Mukavemet Teşkilatı* (TMT/Turkish Resistance Organisation), led by Rauf Denktaş. The British were in a bind: EOKA had not been destroyed, they faced a new threat in the form of the TMT, the 1957 Defence White Paper had imposed significant cutbacks and any settlement needed to satisfy British interests without damaging Macmillan ahead of the next general election (which took place in October 1959). In the end, the stalemate was broken by the Greek and Turkish governments. The London Agreement (February 1959) settled the Cyprus question. Cyprus would become independent, and its administration was split between Greek and

Turkish Cypriots in an elaborate system of checks and balances. The British were able to keep their Sovereign Base Areas at Akrotiri and Dhekelia. As French put it, 'Macmillan opted for an imperfect political settlement because it offered the British the certainty that they could quit while they were (just) ahead' (Ibid, p.301). For EOKA, independence fell short of *enosis* but was better than the alternative of a widening Greek-Turkish struggle. Cyprus became independent in August 1960 with Makarios its first President, but intercommunal violence erupted again in 1963. An attempt at *enosis* in 1974 precipitated a Turkish invasion and division of the island that still exists to this day.

The Development of Counterinsurgency Theory in Britain

The British campaigns in Malaya, Kenya and Cyprus, as well as others in Aden, Oman and Borneo, provided plenty of source material for writers interested in the theory and practice of counterinsurgency. Robert Thompson was, as his obituary in *The Times* put it, 'widely regarded on both sides of the Atlantic as the world's leading expert on countering the Mao Tse-tung technique of rural guerrilla insurgency' (*The Times*, 20 May 1992). His reputation largely rests on his book *Defeating Communist Insurgency* (1966), which was based on his experiences in Malaya and as head of the British Advisory Mission in Vietnam (BRIAM) from September 1961 to March 1965. His memoir, *Make for the Hills* (1989), also contains useful reflections on both conflicts.

Thompson set out five basic principles for the counterinsurgent side to follow.

1. The government must have a clear political aim.
2. The government must function in accordance with law.
3. The government must have an overall plan.
4. The government must give priority to defeating the political subversion, not the guerrillas.

5. In the guerrilla phase of an insurgency, a government must secure its base areas first. (Thompson, *Defeating Communist Insurgency*, pp.50–58).

He suggested that these had gradually become clear in Malaya: as David French has noted, it was Thompson's 'seductive' analysis that helped to establish Malaya as the 'model' counterinsurgency operation (French, *The British Way*, p.3). (Incidentally Thompson disliked the term 'counterinsurgency' for the very reason that it suggested that the government were merely reacting to something, rather than taking proactive steps to confront it).

'By preparing for a long haul,' Thompson wrote, 'the government may achieve victory quicker than expected. By seeking quick military victories in insurgent-controlled areas, it will certainly get a long haul for which neither it nor the people may be prepared' (Thompson, *Defeating Communist Insurgency*, p.58). Winning over the people was the objective: Thompson believed that in an insurgency, 80–90 per cent of the population was neutral, and the aim was, therefore, to win over the majority to the government's side. He suggested that there were four stages in a counterinsurgency: 'clearing', 'holding', 'winning' and 'won' (Ibid, p.111). These stages represented the gradual process by which the government would secure its base areas, work outwards and isolate the insurgents from the population. He pointed out that in the propaganda war, the government should develop its own themes, based on 'practical policy' rather than trying to beat the insurgents at their own game (Ibid, p.97). Given that both Malaya and Vietnam involved jungle fighting, it is significant that Thompson maintained that the insurgent in the jungle need not be feared. 'There are no natural jungle fighters', he wrote. 'Even the insurgent has to learn it' (Ibid, p.155).

Thompson himself recognised that Malaya and Vietnam were different. In the former, the British benefited from the fact that Malaya was smaller, more prosperous, better administered and especially that it could be isolated from external support. On the other hand, in Vietnam, there was plenty of recent experience from the French war and the potential scale of US involvement was far greater than that of Britain. He also argued that the Republic of Vietnam (RVN) enjoyed the advantage of dealing with its own people in the insurgency, although here he perhaps erred. In Malaya, the British benefited from the fact that the MCP's appeal was largely contained within the Chinese population. Thompson's time with BRIAM offers an interesting case study of the difficulties involved in translating counterinsurgency theory into practice. Ian Beckett's description of Thompson occupying 'what might be described as a walk-on part' (Beckett, 'Robert Thompson and the British Advisory Mission to South Vietnam', p.41) in the Vietnam story is apt. Peter Busch has argued that BRIAM was the result of a British initiative. It was felt that some contribution to the Cold War struggle against communism was necessary, and that in so doing Anglo–US relations could be improved; but it was also believed that Britain genuinely had something to offer in Vietnam as a result of its experience in Malaya (Busch, 'Supporting the War', p.70). As Paul Cheeseright has written, 'BRIAM would cost very little, its members would have the expertise to play Greeks to the Romans and it would show the US that the UK remained a loyal and sympathetic ally in spite of concerns about the drift of US policy. It offered involvement without engagement' (Cheeseright, 'Involvement without Engagement', p.267). BRIAM was to advise and assist the RVN, but as Busch has noted, its 'impact on the anti-guerrilla campaign was limited' (Busch, *All the Way with JFK?*, pp. 201–202). Busch has pointed out that the Strategic Hamlet Programme, although redolent of the 'New Villages' in Malaya, was not Thompson's idea, although once he accepted it, he came to believe that victory was imminent. This optimistic view turned to pessimism as he realised that the programme was expanding too fast and was scattered over too wide an area. 'It proved quite impossible', he wrote in *Make for the Hills*, 'to get across that the programme should be carried out as an organized methodical campaign to recover and control territory' (p.130). The

RVN's leadership had different interpretations as to what Strategic Hamlets were designed to do: primarily, they saw them as a way of extending political control, rather than emphasising the possibility of economic and social development. Thompson grew disillusioned following the overthrow of Diem and the political instability that followed. Thompson believed that Vietnamese peasants would reject communism, that the South Vietnamese people simply wanted good government, and that what worked in Malaya would work in Vietnam. Unfortunately, he erred on all three counts (Busch, 'Killing the Vietcong', p.156).

Thompson later praised Nixon's policy of Vietnamisation and argued that the conventional invasion launched by the North in 1972 was the greatest tribute to the RVN's progress. He argued that the lack of support given by the US after 1973 meant that defeat was snatched from the jaws of victory. Thompson's analysis impressed Nixon, who sought his advice in 1969. However, Westmoreland described an early effort to learn from Malaya, with Thompson acting as guide: 'so many were the differences between the two situations,' he wrote, 'that we could borrow little outright from the British experience' (Westmoreland, *A Soldier Reports*, p.69). Thompson criticised the US preoccupation with the big unit war in his 1969 study *No Exit from Vietnam*, but in Vietnam, as Westmoreland justifiably noted, 'it was the irregulars that were drawing support from the regulars' (Ibid, p.149).

General Sir Frank Kitson's career included service in Kenya, Malaya and Northern Ireland. Of his published works, the most significant are his account of his service in Kenya, *Gangs and Counter-Gangs* (1960), *Low Intensity Operations: Subversion, Insurgency and Peacekeeping* (1971), his memoir *Bunch of Five* (1977) and *Directing Operations* (1989). Kitson's major contribution to the art of counterinsurgency was in Kenya, where he developed the idea of the counter- or pseudo-gang. As he wrote in *Gangs and Counter-Gangs*, 'We thought that we might get Africans to impersonate gangsters [Mau Mau] as a regular means of getting information'; the same method was also used for offensive purposes, and counter-gangs proved adept at capturing and killing insurgents (p.75). Effective use was also made of 'turned' Mau Mau fighters, who could be put into the field as double agents, allowing loyal forces to increase the number of 'contacts' with insurgents.

As Kitson put it, 'insurgency is not primarily a military activity ....' The aim of the government when trying to counter such a campaign is to regain and retain the allegiance of its people' (Kitson, *Directing Operations*, pp.50–51). He followed the same logic as Galula, that 'the cause' (or lack of a cause that could compete with that of the insurgency) was the major weakness of the counterinsurgent side. 'It is sometimes said that insurgents start with nothing but a cause and grow to strength,' he noted, 'while the counterinsurgents start with everything but a cause and gradually decline in strength to the point of weakness' (Kitson, *Low Intensity Operations*, p.29). Kitson imagined a successful framework for counterinsurgency as being like a picture frame, with a top, bottom and two sides. At the top was the coordinating machinery, at the bottom were actions taken to persuade the people to reject the insurgency and the two sides were an effective intelligence organisation and the rule of law. Kitson recognised that the qualities required for fighting conventional wars were different to those needed for fighting insurgencies. However, he perhaps fell into the same trap as Trinquier and Galula, in assuming that the latter required greater intellectual effort: he wrote that low-intensity operations 'call for just as much knowledge and skill and an even greater degree of intellectual suppleness and subtlety' (Kitson, *Directing Operations*, p.65).

Counterinsurgency in Northern Ireland (1969–2007)

In Northern Ireland, the British armed forces faced a very different challenge because this was a counterinsurgency campaign that took place within the United Kingdom. The army's deployment to Northern Ireland, Operation *Banner*, lasted from 1969 until 2007 and was the longest continuous deployment in British military history. Northern Ireland was two-thirds Protestant and one-third Catholic. Broadly speaking, as David McKittrick and David McVea put it in their *Making Sense of the Troubles* (2000), 'Almost all Protestants voted Unionist but scarcely any Catholics did', since they 'in the main viewed themselves not as British but as Irish.... The heart of the Northern Ireland problem lies in this clash between two competing national aspirations' (pp.1–2). Moreover, Unionist rule was institutionalised at Catholic expense. During the 1960s, a growing Catholic civil rights movement clashed with loyalists and the Royal Ulster Constabulary (RUC). The descent into violence culminated in the August 1969 'battle of the Bogside', in which a loyalist march in Derry resulted in a running battle between Catholics, Protestants and the RUC. Northern Ireland's Prime Minister, James Chichester-Clark (1969–71), reluctantly asked Harold Wilson's government to send in the army to aid the civil power.

Initially, the British deployment was intended to be merely a short-term peacekeeping operation. However, the army's relations with the Catholic community, which were initially good, began to break down. As Richard English has written in his history of the Irish Republican Army (IRA), 'On both sides, Catholic and Protestant, the violence reinforced those very perceptions by which it had been generated.' Traditional republican arguments about the sectarian nature of the northern state and the need for the IRA as defenders of the Catholic community, he argued, had appeared to be vindicated (English, *Armed Struggle*, pp.103–4). The IRA split into two wings. A dissident group, the Provisional IRA (PIRA), affirmed their commitment to the 32 county Irish republic established by the 1919 Dáil; to the policy of abstention from Stormont (the parliament of Northern Ireland), Dublin and London parliaments; and to armed conflict against Britain. The Official IRA (OIRA) also continued to operate, and there was some feuding between the two groups.

The PIRA sought to lure the army into disproportionate reactions, which would cause it to lose support. Indeed, Paul Dixon has noted that it is debatable whether British conduct in Northern Ireland can be described as employing minimum force. Rod Thornton has argued that while the army had been asked to do a difficult job, its actions made its mission more difficult by alienating it from the population, and Brice Dickson has argued that abuses of human rights prolonged the conflict (Dixon, 'Hearts and Minds?', p.455; Thornton, 'Getting it Wrong', pp.73–107; Dickson, 'Counter-Insurgency and Human Rights', p.476). Perhaps the most important incident took place on Friday 3 July 1970, when troops conducted house searches in the Catholic Falls Road district in Belfast. During the 'battle of the Falls' that followed, the army used 1,600 canisters of CS gas to quell rioting. As a result of the escalating violence, the General Officer Commanding (GOC) Northern Ireland Command, Lieutenant-General Ian Freeland, imposed a curfew until 9am on Sunday 5 July, during which time soldiers conducted further house-to-house searches. Five civilians were killed and 18 soldiers were wounded during the battle of the Falls. It marked a turning point, boosting the profile and popularity of the IRA, and presenting the army as an occupying force, rather than a keeper of the peace. As Richard Iron has written, 'In retrospect, it was a grave mistake for the British government and its army to support a local government that was itself part of the problem' (Iron, 'Britain's Longest War', in Marston and Malkasian (eds), *Counterinsurgency in Modern Warfare*, p.159).

The army by now had extensive experience of counterinsurgency as imperial policing. Indeed, in both Belfast and Derry, at least two different units were given banners ordering rioters to disperse which were written in Arabic. However, the army would not be able to employ some of the measures that had been so important to success in Malaya and Kenya. In Northern Ireland, it would be impossible to carry out a resettlement programme, and with the eyes of the world's media upon them, the conduct of the security forces would be in the spotlight. Northern Ireland Prime Minister Brian Faulkner (1971–72) pushed for internment without trial as the solution to the problem of escalating violence. It had been applied successfully between 1956 and 1961, but it also represented something of a last throw of the dice for Stormont. Internment was controversial and led to significant disagreement. The Chief of the General Staff, General Sir Michael Carver, believed that internment should be a last resort. He later wrote in his memoirs that the haste with which it was approved, and the 'feverish atmosphere' in which the final planning took place, helped to account for many of the problems that followed (Carver, *Out of Step: The Memoirs of Field Marshal Lord Carver*, pp.408–409). However, the Heath government (1970–74) approved internment, and Operation *Demetrius* was launched on 9 August 1971. *Demetrius* is usually seen as a failure. In the words of McKittrick and McVea, internment 'came to be almost universally regarded as a misjudgement of historic proportions which inflicted tremendous damage' (McKittrick and McVea, *Making Sense of the Troubles*, p.80). Martin J. McCleery has argued that the quality of the intelligence on which it was based was better than commonly thought, but implementation does seem to have been somewhat clumsy. Many of those arrested were not in the PIRA. Within two days, more than 100 of those arrested had been released, and most of the more than 2,400 people arrested over the six months that followed were held only briefly. Naturally, this was more likely to antagonise the Catholic community than win over hearts and minds. Moreover, *Demetrius* focused entirely on the Catholic community; loyalist paramilitaries were ignored, and it was not until 1973 that the first loyalist was interned. However, McCleery has contended that *Demetrius* was no indiscriminate attack on the nationalist population. Instead, it was based on the assessment that the republican paramilitaries were the main security threat, and the government preferred to avoid any backlash from loyalist hardliners. Importantly, Dublin did not support *Demetrius*, and the border remained a possible escape route (McCleery, 'Debunking the Myths of Operation Demetrius', pp.411–430).

The interrogation methods used by the army and police caused further controversy. Carver later wrote that he and Lieutenant-General Harry Tuzo (GOC, 1971–73) were unaware of the methods being employed, namely wall-standing, hooding, continuous noise, sleep deprivation and food deprivation. The European Commission on Human Rights would conclude in 1976 that the security forces were guilty of torture, while the verdict of the European Court of Human Rights that these methods constituted 'inhuman and degrading treatment' was no less damning for the government (The Republic of Ireland v. The United Kingdom, ECHR, 1978). Both Stormont and Westminster governments seem to have underestimated the backlash that ensued.

The bloodiest year of the Troubles proved to be 1972, with nearly 500 killed that year. Internment was met with a storm of protest, and one march led to the most infamous event of the Troubles. A tough line had been increasingly taken in Derry in 1971, exemplified by the deployment of 1st Battalion, Parachute Regiment (1 Para), in January 1972. On Bloody Sunday, 30 January 1972, soldiers from 1 Para opened fire, killing 13 and wounding another 13, one mortally. In 2010, the Saville Report into these events concluded that the shooting was not premeditated, but that no warning was given before the soldiers opened fire, that the soldiers fired first and that none of those shot posed a threat (British Government, *Report of the Bloody Sunday Inquiry*, 15 June 2010).

London imposed Direct Rule in March 1972. On one hand, this simplified matters by removing Stormont from the equation, but it also reinforced the IRA's narrative that Britain was a colonial occupier. IRA strategy, therefore, sought to undermine British will to govern and to force a withdrawal. They went on the offensive. On 'Bloody Friday' (21 July 1972), they detonated over 20 bombs, killing nine. Bloody Friday opened the door to the security forces taking back control of Catholic no-go areas – thereby removing a major source of strength for the IRA – in Operation *Motorman*. Prior to *Motorman*, the army undertook a huge build-up of force.

During summer 1972, a peak figure of 28,000 soldiers were deployed in Northern Ireland. A warning was issued ahead of the operation in what would prove to be a successful attempt to minimise civilian casualties. *Motorman* began on 31 July 1972. It was a major operation, involving some 38 battalions in what was, for Britain, the largest deployment of infantry since World War II. It is perhaps an exaggeration to say that *Motorman* effectively transformed the counterinsurgency campaign into a counter-terrorist one. However, as M. L. R. Smith and Peter R. Neumann have noted, in purely statistical terms *Motorman* was the pinnacle of the conflict, and it was followed by a sharp fall in the numbers of bomb attacks, shooting incidents and in the numbers of British servicemen killed (Smith and Neumann, 'Motorman's Long Journey', p.426). Almost half of those killed in the conflict died in the period 1971–76 (1,822 dead). However, as Paul Dixon points out, it is open to question whether coercion resulted in a fall in violence or whether the political climate (such as the imposition of direct rule and the openness to negotiation) created the circumstances in which *Motorman* could be successful (Dixon, 'Hearts and Minds?', p.460).

The conflict was now locked in a stalemate, in which both sides knew they would not be able to inflict military defeat on the other. Indeed, the case of Northern Ireland shows the way in which the political and military aspects of counterinsurgency interrelate with one another, with the military effort being closely linked (on all sides) to the progress of negotiations. Indeed, Dixon argues that classical counterinsurgency theory, which insists that the government needs to demonstrate its political will, cannot account for the success of the peace process, in which concessions were made during negotiations with the IRA (Ibid, pp.472–473). The example of Margaret Thatcher's premiership, as Peter R. Neumann has written, 'shows that even when there was an overwhelming political desire, the existing political and constitutional parameters limited the military options that could be pursued' (Neumann, *Britain's Long War*, p.129). Counterinsurgency operations fell into two categories.

First, overt 'framework' operations included routine measures such as patrolling, searches and manning of checkpoints. The term came into being in the 1980s, but the measures it described were developed much earlier. Second, covert operations were generally undertaken by specialist units. The Special Air Service (SAS), made famous by their rescue of hostages in the 1980 Iranian Embassy siege, were deployed in Northern Ireland from 1976. Perhaps the most notable operation was the Loughgall Ambush (8 May 1987), in which the SAS killed eight volunteers; the IRA's biggest loss of life in a single incident during the Troubles. As David Charters has noted, perhaps more than any other British counterinsurgency campaign, Operation *Banner* became 'intelligence-led' and 'intelligence-driven' (Charters, 'Counter-Insurgency Intelligence', p.64), although this did not happen immediately or without difficulty. However, there were incidents of collusion between the security forces and loyalist paramilitaries, perhaps most notably in the 1989 murder of the Belfast solicitor Pat Finucane.

The reduction in violence in the late 1970s made possible the policies of 'Ulsterisation' (a return to police primacy) and 'criminalisation', which brought an end to the special status paramilitary prisoners had enjoyed. The latter led to a series of prisoner protests, culminating in the famous hunger strikes of 1980–81. Bobby Sands began his hunger strike on 1 March 1981, and won the 9 April 1981 Fermanagh and South Tyrone by-election; a major coup for the IRA. His death on 5 May 1981 caused widespread rioting, and his funeral was attended by 100,000 people. The military stalemate also caused the IRA to reassess their strategy. They adopted a 'long war' approach; a strategy of exhaustion rather than an effort to win outright victory. On 27 August 1979, the IRA detonated two bombs at Warrenpoint, killing 18 soldiers (the deadliest attack on the army during the Troubles) and blew up Lord Mountbatten's fishing boat, killing him and two others. The Sands by-election victory showed the possibilities of an 'Armalite and ballot box' strategy. In the 1983 general election, Sinn Féin won over 100,000 votes, with

Gerry Adams, leader of Sinn Féin from November 1983 until 2018, elected MP for Belfast West. As Dixon points out, it is questionable whether republican 'hearts and minds' were ever won over, given that Sinn Féin became the dominant force in elections once it decided to contest them. The IRA's bombing campaign included military, political and economic targets (such as attacks on soldiers in Hyde Park and Regents Park in July 1982, or the attempt to assassinate Thatcher in Brighton in 1984), but civilian casualties were highly damaging to the IRA's cause (notable examples include the La Mon House bombing in February 1978; Enniskillen in November 1987; and Omagh in August 1998, the deadliest single event of the Troubles in which 29 people were killed). The IRA proved adept at arms procurement and remained well stocked until the end of the campaign. Libya was an important source, although the capture of the ship *Eksund*, carrying a shipment of arms, in autumn 1987 was a major setback. Decommissioning was one of the major issues that remained outstanding following the Good Friday Agreement on 10 April 1998. Following the St Andrews Agreement (2006), restoring power-sharing and the Northern Ireland Assembly, Operation *Banner* formally came to an end on 31 July 2007.

Conclusion

Malaya is seen as the paradigmatic example of British success. Certainly, the British were able to defeat the communist insurgency there. However, the Malayan case study should not be decontextual-ised and its 'lessons' raided for present day use: counterinsurgency operations today take place in very different circumstances. One highly significant factor is that Malaya was part of the British Empire and, therefore, the necessary governmental structures were already in place. Indeed, the era of Malaya and Kenya passed away with the end of empire. In this respect, Vietnam represented the future, in which US forces waged counterinsurgency in a 'host' country. Moreover, the ability to promise independence was a major ace in

Britain's hand in Malaya; no such political solution was possible in the post-9/11 counterinsurgencies in Afghanistan and Iraq. The use of counterinsurgency theory from the period of colonial warfare against communist insurgency within the British and French Empires should also be treated with the same caution. As Gian Gentile has written: 'the ways to counter these wars of revolution as conceived by writers like Galula, Thompson, and Trinquier were specific to the time, place, and context in which they were written. Such books and writings should be seen as primary texts and not as contemporary analyses offering templates for action in current and future wars of insurgency' (Gentile, 'American Counterinsurgency Doctrine', p.28).

Furthermore, the idea of a 'British way in counterinsurgency' can be questioned. The British were willing to use force and sought to hold on in Malaya, Kenya and Cyprus for as long as possible. In particular, the counterinsurgency in Kenya showed that the British were willing to employ more extreme measures in order to win. One would look in vain here for much evidence of 'minimum force', and the use of exemplary force in the British case deserves more attention from historians. Northern Ireland presents a somewhat different case study. Here the British army was deployed on home soil. This constrained what counterinsurgency could achieve, although controversy over the role of the army in the Troubles is unlikely to go away.

CHAPTER 4

Modern Counterinsurgency: Iraq and Afghanistan, 2001–14

Saddam modeled the Ba'ath party on Hitler's Nazi party. Party members, though only 10% of the population, held all key government positions. They ran all political and social institutions, even sports teams. Every Iraqi neighborhood had a party cell to report on neighbors. Like the Nazis, the party recruited children to spy and inform on their parents. Opposition was ruthlessly punished.

PAUL BREMER, HEAD OF THE COALITION PROVISIONAL AUTHORITY IRAQ, *THE GUARDIAN*, 6 JULY 2016

A friction exists between the principles that an intervening counterinsurgent force fights for and the pragmatic steps it must take to avoid inflaming the situation. Sensitivity to the culture and ways of the 'host nation' are important if security is to be established and a lasting political solution reached. But there are always red lines, laid down by policy, which cannot be crossed. The practicality and implementation of these red lines can profoundly influence whole campaigns. In 2003, George W. Bush's administration spearheaded the policy of de-Ba'athification; the removal of the top four tiers of the Iraqi Ba'ath party from any public roles. This was to be implemented by the new Coalition Provisional Authority (CPA) headed by Ambassador Paul 'Jerry' Bremer. Security personnel, civil servants, civic planners and teachers from primary school to university were targeted by the order. Issued 16 May 2003, it was the first order to be passed by the new authority. Somewhere between 35,000 and 40,000 individuals were removed from their posts for their affiliation with Saddam Hussein's regime. The warnings that many of these people were simply professionals trying to further their careers under the harsh conditions of an authoritarian regime were addressed by loose provisions for the programme's 'flexible' implementation. It was inconceivable to the administration that Ba'athists might emerge from the invasion with influence. Detailed pre-war planning was lacking and the power base was absent for its imposition. CPA Order No. 1 was followed up by Order No. 2 to disband the Iraqi Army on 23 May 2003. Within days of George W. Bush's 'Mission Accomplished' speech, the CPA had ordered the effective dissolution of the apparatus of the Ba'athist Iraqi state. The effects of these decisions remain disputed, but critics conclude that it hampered reconstruction efforts, exacerbated the sectarian schism between Sunni and Shia in the country and con- tributed to the rise of a nationalist, Sunni, insurgency. Bremer's words provide an insight into the Manichean mindset of the main drivers behind the policy. Such a black-and-white view left little scope for the grey pragmatism of the British diplomats. The principle behind the policy was what mattered.

The Invasion of Afghanistan (2001)

The attacks of 11 September 2001 produced a decisive shift in US foreign policy. The Taliban regime in Afghanistan had long been implicated in the harbouring of Osama bin Laden. After the Nairobi and Dar-es-Salaam embassy attacks in 1998, the head of the Taliban, Mullah Omar refused to acquiesce to US demands to hand over the head of al-Qaeda. Excuses were offered; *nanawatai* – the Pashtun custom of giving refuge in your own home to those in dire need – was invoked. The Taliban's attempts to negotiate a compromise deal were rebuffed by the United States who demanded his unconditional surrender. Attempts by Prince Turki al-Faisal of Saudi Arabia failed in the face of Mullah Omar's support for bin Laden. Further efforts were hampered by the victory of the Republican party in the 2000 election, bringing George W. Bush to power with a new set of foreign policy objectives. In the meantime, rivalry between the FBI and CIA hampered efforts to halt al-Qaeda's increasingly sophisticated plot. The 11 September attacks immediately brought home the danger of Islamist terrorism. Nine days later, in a speech to Congress, President Bush delivered an ultimatum to Afghanistan:

> In Afghanistan we see al-Qaeda's vision for the world. Afghanistan's people have been brutalised, many are starving and many have fled...By aiding and abetting murder, the Taliban regime is committing murder. And tonight the United States of America makes the following demands on the Taliban: Deliver to the United States authorities all of the leaders of al Qaeda who hide in your land.

Further demands were made, to free foreign hostages, protect journalists, close the terrorist training camps and provide the US full access. The speech, however, is perhaps best known for one line: 'Our war on terror begins with al Qaeda, but it does not end there.' Bush continued, 'It will not end until every terrorist group of global reach has been found, stopped and defeated' (Selected Speeches of President George W. Bush, pp.67–68). That day the British Prime Minister, Tony Blair, was in Congress to send a decisive message. Britain would stand shoulder to shoulder with the US in its new 'war on terror'.

The first airstrikes hit Afghanistan on 7 October after a rapid military and diplomatic effort to prepare. The country offered significant challenges: it was landlocked and there were few airbases to launch strikes from, while the ground forces would, by necessity, be predominantly local groups, such as the Northern Alliance, arrayed against the Taliban supported by special forces, Rangers and Marines. Initially, the airstrikes yielded limited results, but as their intensity grew and negotiations with the anti-Taliban coalition progressed, gains began to be made. By 10 November, the

Northern Alliance forces, headed up by Abdul Rashid Dostum and Atta Mohammed Noor, had captured Mazar-e-Sharif. Soon after Taloqan, Kunduz and Bamiyan fell. By 14 November, the Northern Alliance troops were entering the capital, Kabul. In the south of the country, British Special Forces launched attacks on Taliban forces to cause moral shock, while the US began to negotiate with the local tribes to promote a general uprising against Omar's crumbling regime. Air power crushed Taliban attempts at counter-attack. On 26 October, Abdul Haq was killed by the Taliban. He had emerged as the man most likely to unite Afghanistan's different ethnic and tribal groups. His loss left a vacuum into which Hamid Karzai emerged as a compromise candidate. By the end of November 2001, the Bonn Conference outlined the shape of the new Afghan

The Tora Bora cave complex lies in the Spīn Ghar (Safīd Kūh in Dari) mountain range. In November 2001 the CIA directed airstrikes onto Taliban and al-Qaeda positions but it would take until 20 December for the 2000 Afghan, British and US forces to finally clear the network of tunnels and caves. By the time the complex was cleared, key members of al-Qaeda's hierarchy had escaped, including Osama bin Laden. Pictured here in 2009, Tora Bora continues to be a contested area. (U.S. Department of Defense)

administration. When Kandahar fell on 7 December, the Taliban regime had effectively collapsed. Peace efforts were made, but the US refused to compromise: Mullah Omar was to be surrendered. The Taliban fled, with the majority slipping into Pakistan.

As major operations began to wind down in early 2002, the Taliban started the slow and difficult process of reuniting and rebuilding. As Antonio Giustozzi has shown in *Koran, Kalashnikov and Laptop* (2007), the Afghan insurgency grew steadily between 2002 and 2005. The remnants of the Taliban spent much of the first year divided, but by September, they began to regroup in the North-West Frontier Province of Pakistan (now Khyber Pakhtunkhwa). The structure of the new Karzai regime created instability by building itself upon a network of regional powerbrokers whose allegiance was fickle or dependent upon corruption and nepotism. 'Tribal entrepreneurs' as Giustozzi described them, exaggerated their influence to receive provincial appointments then failed to act as unifying influences. Increasingly, power fragmented and ethnic or tribal loyalties overrode loyalty to the Afghan government. Karzai's regime struggled for legitimacy. Between 2002 and 2006, the Taliban's numbers steadily swelled. The fundamentalist core more than doubled from 3,000 to 7,000 fighters. Locally recruited Afghan insurgents multiplied ten-fold during the same period, reaching 10,000. Foreign support, particularly from Pakistan, bolstered the numbers further. The Taliban slowly infiltrated border provinces in the south and east of the country, and Karzai's control was eroded further. Even before the British entered Helmand province in 2006, attacks on Afghan and International Security Assistance Force (ISAF) personnel had spiked. The stage was set for some of the fiercest fighting Britain's forces would face in the War on Terror.

The Road to Iraq (2003)

As the initial destruction of the Taliban state was being completed in November 2001, US Central Command's (CENTCOM) General

Tommy Franks was ordered to prepare a plan for the invasion of Iraq. On 29 January 2002, President Bush gave his State of the Union address. He turned his aim at the states who 'sponsor terror ... with weapons of mass destruction'. North Korea, Iran and Iraq were in Bush's sights: 'States like these and their terrorist allies constitute an axis of evil, arming to threaten the peace of the world' (Selected Speeches of President George W. Bush, pp.105–106). Tony Blair shared a similar concern with the potential cooperation of WMD armed states and terrorist organisations. The policy of standing 'shoulder to shoulder' with the United States had often masked the sincerity of his own position. As he laid out in his 2010 memoirs, 'if there was a message to be sent about defiance of the international community, it should be sent to Iraq ... If there was a people in need of liberation, it was surely the Iraqi people' (Blair, *A Journey*, p.389).

There were many political twists and turns during 2002 as the US and UK attempted to rally support for a hardline approach to Saddam Hussein's Iraq. The obfuscation and intransigence of Saddam Hussein, coupled with the Bush administration's refusal to accept the compromises that might come with a drawn-out diplomatic process, brought the prospects of a military invasion ever closer. Blair has since, somewhat optimistically, insisted that 'even late in 2002 and early 2003, we could still have avoided a conflict' (Ibid, p.399). The reality was that once Saddam was judged by Washington to have failed to fully meet the demands of the UN's first resolution 1441 (issued in November 2002), the United States was satisfied that military action was justified. Many international partners did not agree. The presentation by the US Secretary of State, Colin Powell, to the UN Security Council on 5 February 2003 was openly challenged by Hans Blix, the UN Chief Weapons Inspector, just over a week later. Russia, France and Germany took sharp stands against the conflict. On 10 March, France threatened to use its UN Security Council veto to halt any second resolution that might demand military action. This effectively torpedoed the prospect of any further UN backing for action. It became clear to many in Washington that they would have to make do with the justification for war provided by the first UN resolution.

The legitimacy of the 2003 invasion hinged upon the ability of the Bush and Blair administrations to present a case that Iraq was harbouring WMDs that had the capability of threatening the safety of the American or British people. For the United Kingdom, one critical moment came with the publication in 2002 of the *September Dossier* (British Government, *Iraq's Weapons of Mass Destruction*). This was principally based upon assessments provided by the Joint Intelligence Committee (JIC). The document itself has become infamous for its claims that Saddam might be capable of launching an attack in 45 minutes. For critics, the dossier has become evidence of Number 10's willingness to manipulate or exaggerate the intelligence picture to make the case for war. The Iraq Inquiry (better known as the Chilcot Report) dismantled this suggestion, concluding that: 'There is no evidence that intelligence was improperly included in the dossier or that No. 10 improperly influenced the text' (Chilcot et al., *Report of the Iraq Inquiry*, p.73). The failure was one of managing the uncertainty of intelligence and the assumptions based upon fragments of evidence drawn from the pre-invasion situation in Iraq. In other words, the British government overlooked qualifications and uncertainties in the JIC assessments to present a case that was far less robust than it seemed. In the long term, this damaged public support for the war and trust in the government.

Despite major protests against the impending war through late 2002 and early 2003, there was a slight majority in favour of the invasion. In the US (*USA Today*/CNN/Gallup) and UK (You Gov) polls showed those supporting military action sat at 58 per cent and 54 per cent respectively. Yet, in 2004, public support in the United Kingdom had plummeted. Contrary to Blair's optimism, the Labour government was never able to restore British support for its participation in Iraq. As a short campaign became bogged down in a maelstrom of sectarian violence with coalition forces caught at the centre of it, the public acceptance of continued sacrifices rapidly diminished. As Christopher Elliott has demonstrated in *High Command* (2015), this created competing strategic demands. The instability required a greater commitment in personnel and resources to improve the situation in southern Iraq. However, with limited public support, the government came under increasing pressure to reduce its 'footprint'. Military commanders were increasingly being asked to do more with less.

The prospect of war had divided the Labour Cabinet. The Foreign Secretary, Jack Straw, harboured reservations throughout and was worried by the language of 'regime change'. Perhaps the fiercest critic was Clare Short, the minister in charge of the Department for International Development (DFID). In March 2003, she had declared the 'whole atmosphere of the current crisis is deeply reckless, reckless for the world, reckless for the undermining of the UN ... reckless with our government, reckless with his [Tony Blair's] own future, position and place in history.' (Andrew Rawnsley interviewing Clare Short, *The Westminster Hour*, BBC Radio 4, 9 March 2003) Her strong stance against the way Blair and Bush were pursuing their diplomacy led her to limit her department's involvement in the post-war planning process. A lack of trust between Number 10 and the DFID had already shown itself the previous year when it had taken until September 2002 for Short's department to be brought into the loop for post-war planning. Once there, the fundamental worries made Short a reluctant participant. The divided Cabinet subverted the traditional mechanism of British government. Rather than calling upon the collective opinions to endorse particular policies, Blair relied on informal or ad hoc arrangements hammered out in private one-to-one meetings. The Chilcot Report subsequently concluded that 'where policy options include significant military deployments ... the options should be considered by a group of Ministers meeting regularly' (Chilcot et al., *Report of the Iraq Inquiry*, p.57). It went on to warn that without full Cabinet meetings, the government might lack 'some external challenge from experienced members of the government' (Ibid, p.57). The inclusion of senior Cabinet members might 'mitigate any tendency towards group-think' (Ibid, p.57). Thus, before a shot was fired, the British and Americans entered the conflict with significant organisational and political weaknesses. The population generally supported action, but the existence of a highly vocal opposition would place pressure on both sides of the Atlantic to find the weapons of mass destruction and establish the brighter future for the Iraqi people.

The Invasion of Iraq (2003)

The main invasion of Iraq began on 20 March 2003. It opened with an impromptu surprise air attack on Dora Farms, where intelligence suggested Saddam was meeting with senior Ba'athists. The information proved inaccurate, and to avoid exposing the ground troops in Kuwait to retaliation, the principal attack was moved forward by 24 hours. Unlike the first Gulf War of 1991, which was preceded by a prolonged and systematic air campaign, the coalition ground offensive followed the opening air strikes more rapidly. The original plan was for a two-day air assault, followed by the land campaign. This would rapidly neutralise the Iraqi air defences, as well as their command and control, while seizing key positions of operational importance. In 1991, the centralised command structure of the authoritarian regime had proven vulnerable to attacks of speed and intensity. The need to pass orders up and down the chain of command left the Iraqi Army unable to cope with the continuously evolving series of attacks. Despite a similar struggle for the Iraqis in 2003, the coalition forces faced significant pockets of resistance. Saddam's Fedayeen, an irregular body of Ba'athist guerrillas, proved to be some of the most difficult to overcome. These 'men of sacrifice' sited their defence around Iraq's cities and employed ambush tactics to hit small unsuspecting groups of coalition soldiers or raided the slower moving convoys. These entrenched militias posed a significant problem for the 1st Marine Division (US) who encountered them in the southern Iraqi city of Nasiriyah. The ferocity of the fighting was evocatively captured by Nathaniel Fick, a Marine Corps officer serving in the 1st Recon Battalion at the time, in his memoir *One Bullet Away* (2005):

> We had stumbled onto the set of a Vietnam movie. Dense green palms encircled us, and a fence of dried fronds lined the side of the clearing. Gunfire echoed everywhere, and Marines darted back and forth, hunched low. Cobras thumped overhead, launching rockets into buildings along the far side of the river. I half-expected the notes of 'Fortunate Son' to come drifting through the trees. (p.205)

These tricky urban engagements provided a foretaste of some of the fighting that would take place during the later emergency in cities like Fallujah.

British forces would be tasked with securing the 'Basra Box', which covered the south-east of the country along the Iranian border up to the city of Al-Amarah. The terrain in the south was a mixture of desert intersected by oil pipelines with limited crossing points. To the north, lay the Maysan marshes. This made the use of heavy vehicles extremely difficult in some areas. The main city in the region was Basra, and it would fall to 7 Brigade to engage the armoured forces Iraq was suspected to have in the area. The plan, however, did not call on British troops to directly attack Basra immediately but to form a cordon around it until the American push on Baghdad developed. This was not a siege: civilians were permitted to move across the British lines. Instead, British troops established a series of checkpoints at key positions across the Basra canal to the west of the city. Any resistance would be met by strike teams based close to these positions. Alongside 1st (United Kingdom) Division, a team of Royal Marines, Polish GROM and US Navy Seals had been tasked with the capture of the Al Faw peninsula, which was the site of a major refinery. Special forces teams from the Special Air Service and US Delta Force went in prior to the coalition ground offensive. Their roles included hunting down Scud missile launchers and providing intelligence of the Iraqi dispositions ahead of the main body of the invasion. Similar to the US Marines operating in Nasiriyah, the British forces began to meet increasing resistance from Saddam's Fedayeen. Opposition hardened along the Basra canal and, particularly, in the town of Zubayr. To combat the growing Fedayeen presence, the British adopted an aggressive raiding strategy. Armoured thrusts were made into Zubayr between 23 March and 1 April. As the intelligence picture improved, Fedayeen strong points were successfully attacked and, by the end of the month, resistance had collapsed. To the north, the forces controlling the crossings of the Basra canal faced increasing attack by small arms, mortar and rocket-propelled grenade (RPG) fire from the east. The Fedayeen's aim was to encourage immediate sallies across the canal that might then be ambushed. Instead, the British took their time and employed a similar policy of aggressive raiding as used in Zubayr. Using Challenger 2 tanks, the British were able to exert greater control over Basra. By 4 April, with Baghdad airport under US control and the capital besieged, the British planned to capture the town of Ad Dayr to the north and move in to secure Basra. With the impending fall of Baghdad looking likely, resistance became more disorganised in the south. Exploiting this, the planned timeline for the operation was accelerated, and after hard fighting on 6 April 2003, the city fell into British hands. On 7 April 2003, cheering crowds of Iraqis were on the streets to welcome the British forces. An officer of the 3 Battalion the Parachute Regiment was quoted as saying in Ripley's *Operation Telic*: 'Despite press cynicism over the term "liberation" we saw it in Basra and it was real' (Ripley, *Operation Telic*, p.148).

By mid-April, the coalition forces had control of Baghdad and Tikrit. Sporadic fighting continued to occur, but at the end of the month, President George W. Bush would land on the USS *Abraham Lincoln* to make his, now infamous, 'Mission Accomplished' speech. The true conflict was only just beginning. There were many driving factors behind the slide towards insurgency but four are notable. The first was a failure of political planning and organisation between all invested parties. Second was the underlying sectarian divide that existed between the Sunni and Shi'ite populations. Third, the presence of foreign 'occupiers' was a catalyst for rebellion and pulled the coalition in different directions. The final factor was the breakdown of security and basic provision at street level. These elements intertwined to create a perfect storm of conditions for an embryonic insurgency. Further inflaming matters was a small but growing al-Qaeda contingent under the direction of Abu Musab al-Zarqawi. These fighters, mostly of foreign origin, collected under the banner of al-Qaeda in Iraq (AQI) from October 2004. They would be responsible for many terrorist attacks directed at the Shi'ite population in order to elicit a violent response. AQI's goal was to create a sectarian civil war in Iraq.

The political failure started before a gun was fired. The Chilcot Report concluded that Number 10 had made assumptions about how the post-war reconstruction of Iraq would be managed. They had presupposed that the post-war plan would be drawn up by the US; the UN Security Council would authorise any 'post-conflict activity'; and that international partners would contribute to the rebuilding effort. When the US showed reluctance to hand over the post-invasion administration to the UN, the UK was left to compromise that the UN would authorise the coalition's administration. The actual planning for the stabilisation of Iraq fell principally upon the US, which limited the UK's influence. Yet, as Chilcot concludes, the major government ministries could have done more. The Foreign and Commonwealth Office (FCO) lacked resources and experience of 'nation-building of the scale required in Iraq, and did not expect to do so' (Chilcot et al., *Report of the Iraq Inquiry*, p.81) according to the Iraq Inquiry. DFID limited its engagement to humanitarian needs created by the invasion and little beyond it. While the Ministry of Defence (MOD) flagged the importance of stabilisation and reconstruction, it required the government to coordinate the involvement of the other two ministries. By the time of the invasion, these problems remained effectively unresolved and doubts hung over the US team responsible, initially, for post-war planning – the Office of Reconstruction and Humanitarian Aid (ORHA). There was little appetite within the UN to take on the responsibility of reconstructing Iraq and the Americans remained sceptical. This, Chilcot concluded: 'increased the risk that the UK would be unable to respond to the unexpected in Iraq' and 'In the longer term, they reduced the likelihood of achieving the UK's strategic objectives in Iraq' (Ibid, p.86).

The situation was made worse by divisions that lurked inside the Cabinet over the legitimacy of military action. The Leader of the Commons, Robin Cook, resigned in March 2003 over the invasion, and in May, Clare Short stood down from her role. To rationalise the government's response, the Ad Hoc Ministerial Group on Iraq Rehabilitation (AHMGIR) was established in April 2003, which was chaired by the Foreign Secretary, Jack Straw. This brought some degree of coordination, but by that point, the invasion was already under way and problems were arising. The UK succeeded in its compromise of the UN authorising the coalition's administration in Iraq. In mid-May, UN Security Council Resolution 1483 was passed, which attempted to establish the responsibilities of the 'occupying powers' and set up UN support for humanitarian relief. It abolished the Oil-for-Food Programme. It also handed authority to the newly established CPA to use Iraq's oil revenues to aid in the country's reconstruction. This did not give the United States or the United Kingdom carte blanche to exploit the country's oil reserves. In fact, the UK's preferred position was for an Iraqi-led body, the UN or the World Bank to control oil revenues. The CPA was required by the resolution only to authorise expenditure to aid the Iraqi people. The UN had also agreed to send a team to Baghdad under Sérgio Vieira de Mello, who was acting as Special Representative to the UN Secretary-General, Kofi Annan. In August 2003, the UN Headquarters was attacked by a suicide bomber operating under the banner of *Jama'at al-Tawhid wal Jihad*; the precursor group to what would become al-Qaeda in Iraq. The attack killed Mello and the UN moved their team to Jordan.

The divisions and failures of planning led to uncertainties on the ground. Once British forces moved into Basra, they faced widespread Iraqi looting and lawlessness. Inadequate planning left deep uncertainties over the rules of engagement when dealing with looters. British commanders were forced to adapt on the fly. Brigadier Graham Binns, commanding 7 Armoured Brigade in Basra, told the Iraq Inquiry: 'the best way to stop looting was just to get to a point where there was nothing left to loot' (Ibid, p.87). The problems were magnified in US-controlled Baghdad. Paul Bremer recalled a conversation with Clay McManaway, deputy at the CPA, in *My Year in Iraq: The Struggle to Build a Future of Hope* (2006) where the situation was described as 'industrial-strength looting' and that 'after they strip a place they torch it. Lots of old scores to settle' (p.3). The CPA's policies exacerbated the situation. The decision to disband the security forces and slow progress in retraining Iraqi police officers demonstrated a distinct lack of flexibility and pragmatism. The wave of instability critically damaged infrastructure and, in turn, undermined the fragile relationship between the occupiers and the occupied. To compound this problem, Britain had planned to reduce its deployment in the south of Iraq from 46,000 to between 25,000–30,000 personnel. By the end of May 2003, this had fallen to 18,000. The expectation was that other nations would increase their contributions, and while 5,000 troops from nine countries were committed in summer 2003, Britain

---

British Troop Numbers in Iraq 2003–9 (according to MOD figures)

Invasion 2003: 46,000	May 2006: 7,200
May 2003: 18,000	May 2007: 5,500
May 2004: 8,600	May 2008: 4,100*
May 2005: 8,500	May 2009: 4,100*

*In southern Iraq only.

was forced to increase numbers in September. This was a minor increase against a general trend of slow withdrawal.

Instability in Iraq was most noticeable in the centre of the country and in Baghdad. In June 2003, there was an almost complete breakdown of vital infrastructure. Food shortages, electricity blackouts and a lack of clean water inflamed nationalist sentiment. CPA projections at the end of May put power generation for the country at 300MW against a need of 6,000MW. Estimates suggested it would take until the end of September for power to reach pre-war levels of 4,000MW, still well below the number needed for the country. Jobs were scarce and unemployment was high. The circumstances were not yet favourable for establishing a strong market economy, overturning Saddam's planned economy. The CPA's first two orders made this much worse. Hundreds of thousands of former soldiers and civil servants caught up in the de-Ba'athification process and security sector reforms were pushed into a labour market that was devoid of opportunity. Many had access to firearms and the training to use them; crime predictably skyrocketed. Some sought retribution against the coalition. Consequently, the CPA's first two policies were a powerful recruiting tool for insurgent groups.

Politically, there remained no firm resolution over the establishment of a new Iraqi-led government or authority. This did much to inflame the relationship between the coalition forces and the people. On 22 and 24 June 2003, attacks were launched on UK forces in Majar al-Kabir in Maysan. In Baghdad, small arms and RPG attacks were increasing in number. Meanwhile, the CPA was still attempting to organise an interim Iraqi government. After a US/UK vetting process, the Iraqi Governing Council was formed from representatives of the major ethnic and religious groups. The group consisted predominantly of Shias, with representation for Sunnis, Kurds, Turkmens and Assyrians. Three of the representatives were women. The group convened on 13 July 2003 and they were to drive the formulation of a new constitution. It would take another year before the Governing Council was replaced by the

Iraq: A Divided Nation?

Iraq is a heterogenous society. Most of the population are Shia (66 per cent) with just under 30 per cent being Sunni. There are multiple ethnicities including Arab, Persian, Kurd, Assyrian and Turkmen. Frequently these groupings overlap. Sunni and Shia with a shared Arab background intermarried, particularly in the more cosmopolitan cities. Despite this, Saddam's rule had left Iraq's politics and society divided along ethnic, religious and tribal lines. Sunni dominance under the Ba'ath Party was replaced by Shia pre-eminence in post-invasion Iraq. The deposed Ba'athists and Fedayeen moved to rally Sunnis fearful of losing their status. Al-Qaeda in Iraq drew in fighters from Saudi Arabia and the wider Middle East. Shia militias, such as *Jaysh al-Mahdi* under the direction of Muqtada al-Sadr, attracted young disaffected men to their cause. The coalition had to operate in an increasingly fractured society.

Iraqi Interim Government and Iraq would not have a permanent, democratically elected government until 2006. Dealing with these bodies was often a case of cajoling and compromise. Pulled in different ways by the demands of their community, the Governing Council was neither truly independent – it relied on the coalition for security – nor a mere puppet, complicating coalition efforts to soften the de-Ba'athification rules.

2003 was a year of mixed fortunes. In the US-controlled areas, increasing violence was met with a hard-line approach in most provinces. After the invasion, General Tommy Franks retired. He was replaced at CENTCOM by General John Abizaid, while Lieutenant-General Ricardo Sanchez assumed command on the ground in Iraq, leading all coalition forces in theatre under the new Combined Joint Task Force 7 (CJTF). As Carter Malkasian has recognised, no centralised counterinsurgency plan was formulated by the new generals, resulting in US divisional commanders taking very different approaches. Major-General Raymond Odierno of 4th Infantry Division was particularly robust, using firepower, large-scale area sweeps and the detainment of family members of known insurgents. At the other end of the spectrum, Major-General David Petraeus of 101st Airborne Division employed a more careful approach in the Nineveh province. Malkasian described how he asked his subordinates before approving offensives: 'Will this operation take more bad guys off the street than it creates by the way it is conducted?' (Malkasian, 'Counterinsurgency in Iraq,' in Marston and Malkasian (eds), *Counterinsurgency in Modern Warfare*, p.289). Sanchez's lack of coordination was, perhaps, more understandable while uncertainties remained over the security situation and opposition, but a more connected plan was required after the bloody spring of 2004.

The time after the invasion proved to be a short honeymoon period for the British forces. Although attacks were increasing, troops were able to take a light approach and tried to avoid antagonising the people they were there to protect. Much of the effort was spent training local Iraqi forces. Things changed in February 2004. A wave of suicide bombings left more than 200 dead. The following month, the attacks quadrupled. On 31 March, four civilian contractors were killed in Fallujah and their bodies were hung from a bridge over the Euphrates. By 4 April, the 1 Marine Expeditionary Force (MEF) had encircled the city and launched raids into it. Over the next five days, the fighting intensified with the Marines using air and artillery strikes to pacify resistance. Civilians were caught in the crossfire; many more thousands were internally displaced. The Marines' attack inflamed Sunni sentiment across Iraq and the Iraqi Governing Council pushed for a temporary ceasefire by threatening to resign. Although, the coalition forces agreed to this, fighting would continue until early May when operations were handed over to CIA-backed, local forces. When these defected, a portion of the city centre was effectively left in the hands of the various Sunni extremist groups. It became an insurgent stronghold from which attacks could be launched around the country. Control would not be restored until the second battle of Fallujah in November and December 2004.

Concurrently, a crisis erupted in central and southern Iraq. After protests and increasingly violent attacks in early March conducted by Muqtada al-Sadr's *Jaysh al-Mahdi* (JAM), a mosque in Kufa was occupied by 60 militiamen on 23 March 2004. The troops in the area were a mix of nationalities but the Spanish, under *General de brigada* Fulgencio Coll Bucher, comprised the main force. The coalition troops were reluctant to be seen to be attacking a mosque. Bremer urged the Spanish troops to take more aggressive action against the JAM who were now setting up roadblocks, kidnapping and torturing Iraqi police. Bremer concluded that the Spanish's 'lack of resolve emboldened Muqtada' (Bremer, *My Year in Iraq*, p.312). He was ignoring the significant shift in Spanish public opinion that had occurred that month. On 11 March, ten explosions ripped through four commuter trains in Madrid leaving 193 people dead and over 2,000 wounded. The attack, which was later claimed by al-Qaeda, seemed to have a dramatic effect on the general election that was due to take place three days later. Spanish public support for the country's involvement in Iraq was low. The country had been targeted by Islamic terrorists and days later the Socialist party, led by José Zapatero, overcame a five per cent deficit in the polls to win the election with a five per cent margin – a ten per cent swing. Prime Minister Zapatero's policy of withdrawal from Iraq, therefore, constrained General Coll, who was under pressure from the new anti-war administration at home and an increasingly belligerent Bremer in Iraq. By 26 March, the JAM were attacking CPA administrative centres across some of the southern cities. That evening, Muqtada al-Sadr delivered an anti-Semitic denunciation of Israel and the coalition in the Kufa mosque, going so far as to praise the perpetrators of the 9/11 attacks. Bremer's response was to order the shut-down of *Al-Hawza*, a Sadrist paper, for 60 days.

The newspaper was accused of encouraging violence against Iraqis cooperating with the coalition and it had published a transcript of al-Sadr's speech. To many Iraqis, it seemed like the Americans were censoring a legitimate outlet of criticism. On 3 April, the protests that followed the closure of the newspaper ignited into violence when Bremer ordered the arrest of Mustafa al-Yacoubi, the editor of *Al-Hawza* and a close ally of Muqtada al-Sadr. Mobs took to the streets with rifles and RPGs.

Following the closure of *Al-Hawza* and the attack on Fallujah, the situation rapidly deteriorated in the south. Eruptions of violence took place as Sadr's supporters poured onto the streets and targeted CPA or coalition buildings. Najaf and the Baghdad suburb of Sadr City became hot points of Shia rebellion against the occupation. Nasiriyah, al-Amarah, Kut and Basra were all affected. Bremer's orders were to tackle the JAM head on. Many coalition partners equivocated, attempted negotiation or took a defensive stance. At a time when Sunni opinion of the coalition and Iraqi Governing Council was at its lowest, with the political reconstruction hanging by a thread, with military forces spread thinly across the country and relying on firepower to maintain its own security, Bremer inflamed Shia opinion and gave Muqtada al-Sadr the excuse he was looking for to escalate to violent rebellion. It was fair of Bremer to assume that a confrontation was always likely. However, his uncompromising approach played into the JAM's hands at a moment of genuine coalition weakness. Moreover, his failure to appraise his coalition partners of his plans to arrest al-Yacoubi left them dangerously unprepared for the backlash that followed. Ripley quotes Brigadier Nick Carter's (later to become General Nick Carter, Chief of the Defence Staff) debrief: 'Had we known we would have at least been able to prepare the ground. The arrest of a Shia religious figure had an impact on the whole of the Shia South with the consequence that my whole Area of Operations went up in smoke' (Ripley, *Operation Telic*, p.203). This was a sentiment that Major-General Andrew Stewart, commanding the Multi-National Division (South East) in

Basra, agreed with. He reported to the Iraq Inquiry that on 6 April 2004 'it was like a switch had been flicked'. It became 'an insurgency overnight' (Chilcot et al., *Report of the Iraq Inquiry*, Vol. 7, p.343; 'Transcript of Sir Hilary Synnott, Lt Gen Lamb, Maj Gen Andrew Stewart hearing', Iraq Inquiry Oral Evidence, 9 December 2009).

In the following months, violence continued to explode with regularity across Iraq. A proliferation of groups influenced events in the south: the Badr Brigade vied for control with JAM and tribal groups, while the Fadhila were nominally political but were considered to be corrupt. In mid-June, under severe pressure from American forces, al-Sadr called a temporary ceasefire. This held until 4 August. That month, renewed attacks by JAM reached the same level as April 2004. Only the intervention of Grand Ayatollah al-Sistani allowed a tentative solution to be brokered between the newly created Iraqi Interim Government and Muqtada al-Sadr at the end of the month. Nonetheless, new hard-line commanders like Ahmed al-Fartosi had risen to positions of prominence within the Sadrist group and were leading attacks on the coalition. It became clear that Iraq's nascent security forces would be in no shape to assume control of their own security until 2006. The US began to rethink their entire strategy in light of the insurgency they now faced. On 28 June, the CPA handed over to the Iraqi Interim Government headed by Prime Minister Ayad Allawi. Soon after, Lieutenant-General Ricardo Sanchez was replaced by General George Casey Jr who conducted a review of operational planning in late 2004. The result was a greater focus on training Iraqi forces and attacking foreign insurgents inside Iraq. The British were drawn in different directions. Domestic opposition to the UK's involvement pushed the government towards a reduction in troop numbers, while the security situation on the ground remained precarious. Furthermore, in June 2004, the Blair government made a commitment to deploy the Allied Rapid Reaction Corps (ARRC) to Afghanistan in 2006. The focus, therefore, progressively shifted theatres; from Iraq towards Afghanistan. In effect, the policy opened a second front at a time when the UK could ill-afford it. This would strain relations between Washington and London, while those deployed on the ground in Basra had to face the consequences of poor resourcing and a resurgent enemy.

Decline and Divergence in Iraq

Starting in late 2004, the US began a process of intellectual and practical reflection that ultimately led to the adoption of a new counterinsurgency doctrine and a fresh approach to Iraq and later Afghanistan. The British would take somewhat longer and reach slightly different conclusions. These changes have not been without criticism, but when considered as a response to the very immediate challenges of the two ongoing conflicts, it is difficult to see what alternative set of principles would have yielded better results. The US and UK theories that emerged were never designed to be definitive 'how-to' guides but to focus the minds of the troops on the problems they would encounter in theatre. Perhaps more important than the theoretical changes were the practical improvements in training, provisioning and organisation that affected later operational tours. Ultimately, any changes in counterinsurgency doctrine could do little if wider political and strategic failures occurred.

General Casey's appointment to command the CJTFF7, renamed the Multi-National Force – Iraq (MNF-I), was followed by an attempt to address the disconnect between the political and military plans for the country. The new US ambassador to Iraq, John Negroponte, worked with Casey to improve security and oversee reconstruction in the country. To do this, experts in counterinsurgency were brought in; Colonel Bill Hix and Kalev Sepp both had special forces backgrounds and expertise in stabilisation operations. Sepp started by looking at over 20 counterinsurgency campaigns in the 20th century to assess best practice. He found that a secure and supportive population coupled with a legitimate government was pivotal to success. It became clear to some in the coalition that the methods used up to that point breached many of Sepp's practices. The coalition's dependence on firepower for troop security, and large search and destroy raids, were undermining their credibility with the Iraqi people. This was particularly felt by the Sunni population. Their disaffection had grown as a result of the CPA's de-Ba'athification and security sector reform orders, which fell disproportionately against them. The US actions in Fallujah only worsened this view. To begin to rectify the situation, intelligence needed to be improved to allow for greater precision in targeting the insurgents, rather than conducting broad sweeps that alienated the innocent caught up in the operations. Systemic problems remained at the higher levels of Iraqi society. A critical disconnect existed between the Iraqi Interim Government and the various ethnic, religious and tribal groups. Many saw the new regime as a puppet of the West. The new government's legitimacy was limited and rested on its ability to co-opt key power brokers and individuals with jobs or favours. Rather than representing all Iraqis, it was increasingly viewed as Shia dominated, inflaming tensions further with the disaffected Sunni minority. Corruption, particularly among the Iraqi Police Force, was a significant problem that showed no sign of resolution in 2005. The new Iraqi Security Forces (ISF) were increasing in size and Casey took steps to improve the US's focus on training. Nonetheless, doubts persisted over their utility and commitment.

To improve the training of the Iraqi forces the Multi-National Security Transition Command – Iraq (MNSTC-I) was established and headed up by Lieutenant-General David Petraeus in June 2004. In the following months, Petraeus and Casey planned to increase the size of the ISF. Police, border officers and the Iraqi National Guard would need to be expanded significantly. The proposed total was 271,000, which required 50 per cent increases to the local Iraqi police and Iraqi National Guard. The Border Force would be doubled in size from 16,000 to 32,000. This became known as the Petraeus Plan. The MNSTC-I replaced civilian contractors training Iraqi forces and gave responsibility to US Army soldiers. It took time for them to adapt to the new role as instructors, and it was recognised that advisers would need specific preparation in the United States before being deployed. In 2006, a new course was established in Fort Riley, Kansas, to do this. Pre-deployment training shifted away from the emphasis on mobile, conventional operations towards a counterinsurgency programme. By 2006, six regional training centres had been established in Iraq to help train non-commissioned officers and three military academies were opened to train commissioned officers. The officer training course was built upon the British curriculum taught at the Royal Military Academy Sandhurst (RMAS).

The British response to the expansion and training changes in the Petraeus Plan was positive at first. Geoff Hoon's Private Secretary, Mike Naworynsky, wrote to Tony Blair's Private Secretary on 20 August 2004 concluding that 'US thinking in this area remains very similar to our own with the key theme of Iraqiisation running through the brief' (Chilcot et al., *Report of the Iraq Inquiry*, Vol. 10, p.178). The reform would form a critical strand of Prime Minister Allawi's Iraqi National Security Strategy. Yet he would take until January 2005 to publish it, leaving doubts over the coalition and Interim Government's management of the steadily deteriorating security situation. Moreover, senior British figures were sceptical about the speed of expansion and the resourcing of the new forces. More worryingly, the drive for symbolic numbers had overshadowed the actual capabilities of the new ISF. Major-General Nick Houghton, Assistant Chief of the Defence Staff (Operations), described the situation in his paper to the Chiefs of Staff on 21 September 2004: 'It is focusing too much on short-term, physical and – to an extent – symbolic representations of capability; it is not focusing enough on the capabilities which will actually allow Iraq to fight its own campaign' (Ibid, p.189) Houghton's point was clearly underlined a month later when 5,000 Iraqi police in Mosul surrendered to insurgents after they coordinated attacks on police stations, forcing coalition troops to intervene. The planned Iraqi elections in 2005, funding difficulties and the focus on quantity over quality undermined the efforts of the coalition and Iraqi Interim Government to create a large, reliable Iraqi Force.

The uptake of counterinsurgency methods across the US forces was inconsistent. During late 2004 and 2005, there were notable successes but US soldiers continued to rely heavily upon firepower. 'Escalation of force' incidents (such as shooting oncoming vehicles) were dangerously commonplace. The killing of 24 Iraqi civilians in November 2005 by Marines in Haditha after they were attacked by a roadside bomb was an extreme example of the violence some US troops employed. There were successes which seemed to signal the future. The second battle of Fallujah, from 7 November until 23 December 2004, cleared the city of remaining AQI insurgents and neutralised the perceived challenge to the new Iraqi Interim Government. However, it further entrenched Sunni disillusionment. After being pushed out of Fallujah, AQI insurgents fled to Al Qa'im, a city of 200,000 inhabitants on the Syrian border. In November 2005, this was cleared by US Marines supported by a battalion of the Iraqi Army in Operation *Steel Curtain*. Afterwards, the Marines integrated within an Iraqi brigade and the Albu Mahal tribesmen were persuaded to support the ISF in the area. In September 2005, Tal Afar was cleared of insurgents by the US 3rd Armored Reconnaissance Regiment and two Iraqi brigades. The city's civilian inhabitants had been warned of the coming offensive and evacuated, allowing Colonel H. R. McMaster, commanding the US forces, to use artillery and air power to attack the insurgents. Rather than simply withdraw after the immediate victory, McMaster spread his forces across the city in 29 separate outposts and limited the use of force.

These actions were seized upon by the Bush administration. 'Clear – hold – build' became a mantra denoting the new strategy. Yet, as an idea, it lacked detail or scalability. The successes of Al Qa'im and Tal Afar were local and depended on regional circumstances; they could not easily be applied across the country. The coalition lacked the troop numbers to adequately clear and hold the populous city suburbs, particularly in Baghdad, and the ISF were not reliable enough to carry out the strategy themselves. Building proved to be difficult, with administrative hurdles created by the labyrinthine bureaucracy of the CPA, then of the Iraqi Interim Government and later Iraqi Transitional Government. This was further complicated by national rules. As Major-General Andrew Stewart observed during the Iraq Inquiry: 'there was no shortage of money, we just couldn't spend it' (Iraq Inquiry Oral Evidence, 9 December 2009).

The political situation in Baghdad created its own set of problems. In January 2005, elections for the National Assembly of Iraq were held. Over 62 per cent of the vote and 180 seats went to Shia parties, while the Kurdish Alliance, with 25 per cent of the vote, took 75. As turnout for the National Assembly elections was low in Sunni areas, Sunni parties only claimed a handful of seats. After a protracted period of negotiation between the various political parties, Ibrahim al-Ja'afari became Prime Minister of the new Iraqi Transitional Government in May, taking over from Ayad Allawi. Ja'afari's government would be responsible for creating and implementing the new Iraqi constitution. On 15 October, Iraqis once more went to the polls to vote on the adoption of the new constitution of Iraq; this passed with 78 per cent voting in favour. Almost from the outset, Ja'afari's tenure as Prime Minister was marked by a progressive breakdown in Sunni/Shia relations within Iraq. The delay in forming the Iraqi Transitional Government and lack of Sunni representation in the Cabinet diminished faith in the competence of the new authority. Violence increased upon the announcement of the new government with 70 attacks a day taking place. By October, 150 bodies a week were being discovered in Baghdad, most of them Sunni Arabs. The British ambassador to Iraq, Edward Chaplin, was quoted in the Chilcot Report as describing, the 'nasty sectarian tinge to much of the killing' (Chilcot et al., *Report of the Iraq Inquiry*, Vol. 7, p.486). The new constitution proved divisive as well. Although it enshrined religious tolerance, Sunnis felt the federal nature of the new state would exclude them from their share of oil revenues; the majority of which lay in Shia or Kurdish areas.

For much of 2005 the situation remained tense. Violence predominantly took place in the Sunni dominated areas of Iraq, although hard-line Shia groups in the south were posing an increasingly sophisticated threat using Iranian-made improvised explosive devices (IEDs). Foreign jihadists moved among their disaffected Iraqi coreligionists, and by July, the British Joint Intelligence Committee concluded that 'Sunni Arab insurgents have no strong reason to turn on the jihadists' (Ibid, p.501) By September, a report by Sir Nigel Sheinwald for Tony Blair recognised the '**increased and vicious sectarianism** [emphasis in original]' (Ibid, p, 524) of the past months was endangering the fragile political balancing act in Iraq. The violence was not confined to Sunni insurgents but also involved 'Shia elements within the police and armed forces, and from the Shia militia' (Ibid, p.524). This had the potential to draw the country into a sectarian civil war and undermine the nascent democratic regime before it had effectively been established. Coincidentally, on the same day Sheinwald's report was given to Blair, two British Special Forces soldiers were arrested in Basra by the Iraqi Police Service (IPS) acting in consort with local Shia militias. The soldiers were beaten and images were broadcast on Arab television. The subsequent crisis led to a British cordon being established and rioting on the streets of Basra. When negotiators moved in to try to arrange for the soldiers' return they were taken hostage. With the threat of escalating violence, a rescue attempt was made which led to the captives' release. The Jameat incident, named after the police station the soldiers were first taken to, underscored the collusion between the Shia militias and the Iraqi authorities. By the end of the month, a JIC report concluded frankly that the: 'Iraqi government has neither the will nor capacity to tackle these problems: this will probably not change after the elections' (Ibid, p.534) During 2005, much of the coalition's political efforts were expended attempting to bridge the divide between the Shia and Sunni communities. There were some limited successes and when the elections for the new permanent Iraqi government took place in

December 2005 the level of Sunni participation dramatically rose. Meetings had taken place between Jack Straw, and the two leading Sunni political coalitions in November 2005 to promote greater involvement. Yet it was also a response to the lessons of the January 2005 Iraqi National Assembly elections that bolstered participation. The January boycott had reduced the Sunni ability to influence Ja'afari's Transitional Government and so they agreed to take part in December to maintain their political standing within Iraq.

Sunni support for the Iraqi elections on 15 December 2005 created an opportunity for reconciliation between some within the insurgency and the political process. Both the US and UK administrations recognised the need to align the military and political efforts. 'Transition' became the key tenet for planning in 2006. As Lieutenant-General Nick Houghton, in his role as Senior British Military Representative and Deputy Commanding General MNF-I, reported to the Chief of the Defence Staff General Sir Michael Walker, 'the principal focus for 2006 should be the support to Transition' (Ibid, p.573). He emphasised that building the Iraqi security forces and their capabilities should be a priority. General Casey, commanding MNF-I, held similar views and withdrew US forces where he felt able to. Events, however, took a marked turn for the worse. After the elections, a period of political uncertainty set in. The alliance of Shia parties had swept to victory but were deeply divided over who would lead the new government. Ja'afari wanted to remain in post but was opposed by the sizable Kurdish faction, the Shia Supreme Council for the Islamic Revolution in Iraq (SCIRI) and George W. Bush, who saw him as a weak and divisive leader. It took four months of political negotiations before a compromise candidate, Nouri al-Maliki, emerged. He was sworn in on 20 May 2006. The stalemate left many Sunnis disenchanted with the political process.

On 22 February 2006, the golden dome of the al-Askari mosque in Samarra, the fourth holiest Shia shrine, was destroyed by AQI insurgents dressed in Iraqi police commando uniforms. Their intent was to inflame sectarian sentiment. Despite a city-wide curfew and the deployment of ISF to holy sites, over 50 mosques were targeted in follow-up attacks. AQI focused on attacking key members of the Shia Badr Corps, a political-military wing of SCIRI, and sectarian violence in Samarra left 119 civilians dead by the end of February. Baghdad rapidly descended into chaos. A Joint Intelligence Committee report of April 2006 made it clear that the violence in some areas had 'gained its own momentum' and the sectarian divisions within the ISF cast doubt upon their cohesion and capability to respond. By May 2006, there were 3,196 attacks, of which 1,000 occurred in Baghdad. Attempts to calm the situation failed. In June, Operation *Together Forward* was launched by the ISF, with the support of coalition troops, but the limited troop numbers meant the policy of 'clear, hold, build' stood little chance of success. August's Operation *Together Forward II* fared little better. Although political assessments denied that Iraq had descended into civil war, on the ground the reality was a rising tide of ethno-sectarian violence. By December, there were over 3,000 Iraqi deaths per month.

Things were not much better in the south of the country. By May 2006, there were between eight and ten assassinations occurring every day in Basra. Sunnis were the primary target. The threat of physical violence, extortion and intimidation hung over the people. Demonstrations against the lack of reliable public services inflamed things further. The provincial authorities showed little inclination to grip the deteriorating security situation. More worryingly for Number 10, their US allies began to harbour doubts about Britain's willingness to continue. As General Mike Jackson, the British Army's Chief of the General Staff, wrote from Baghdad:

> The perception, right or wrong, in some – if not all – US military circles is that the UK is motivated more by the short-term political gain of early withdrawal than by the long-term importance of mission accomplishment; and that as a result, MDN (SE)'s operational posture is too laissez faire and lacks initiative. (Chilcot et al., *Report of the Iraq Inquiry*, Vol. 7, pp.608–9)

That same month the British-led NATO Allied Rapid Reaction Corps deployed to Afghanistan to act as the first NATO in-theatre headquarters. Simultaneously, the UK's 16 Air Assault Brigade deployed to Helmand province in Afghanistan. Britain became engaged in two major operations simultaneously. This breached a critical assumption of their pre-war strategic planning first established by the *Strategic Defence Review* of 1998 and later reaffirmed in the MOD review of 2002. The concurrency of Iraq and Afghanistan from mid-2006 until Britain's withdrawal from Iraq in 2009 strained the army's resources, equipment and personnel. Perhaps more dangerously, it created a strategic imperative for a timely withdrawal from Iraq and increasingly placed them at odds with their US coalition partners.

In August 2006, steps were taken to implement the Iraqi-led Basra Security Plan; the aim of which was to strengthen Iraqi government control and enable the handover of the southern Iraqi provinces to provincial Iraqi control. Discussions took place between Major-General Shirreff, British commander of the Multi-national Division (South East), also known as MND (SE), the Iraqi Major-General Hamadi and the USA's General Casey over political support and resourcing. The final plan that emerged, initially called Operation *Salamanca*, was broadly in-keeping with the US strategy of 'clear, hold, build'. Basra would be cleared, area by area, using British and Iraqi Army troops. They would be followed up by reconstruction teams using Iraqi contractors. The final objective was to shatter the militia presence in Basra, break the JAM's grip on the city and ultimately allow the full handover to the Iraqi authorities. The operation was scheduled to begin in mid-September 2006 and run for six months. However, compromise was baked into the plan from the outset. The US offered to deploy a battalion from the MNF-I's operational reserve, but this was rejected in London who considered the deployment of US troops to be a potentially inflammatory and escalatory move. Instead, an 'uplift' of 350 British troops was requested for a duration of four

Gurkhas on patrol in Helmand. (Sgt Ian Forsyth RLC/MOD)

months, $80 million for reconstruction was secured, along with US intelligence and air assets. The deeper problems lay within Maliki's Iraqi government, which increasingly prevaricated over tackling the militias in Basra. Negotiations over precisely which areas of the city would be targeted initially continued deep into September, and Major-General Shirreff's resolve to bring the militias to heel was fundamentally undercut by Iraqi unwillingness to launch a lasting operation that might ultimately disrupt the fragile political balance of power in the region. The shifting sands of Shia networks of loyalty crushed any potential for lasting change. The scope and scale of the operation was chosen according to what was politically acceptable to Baghdad rather than what was required. Meanwhile, London's careful attention to troop numbers and the deployment of troops to Helmand curtailed any chance of the British going it alone. There was a growing fear that British troops were a cause rather than a cure for instability.

Before the operation was launched on 28 September 2006, it was renamed Operation *Sinbad*. The initial results were positive.

British and Iraqi troops successfully pacified parts of Basra but, in response, the militias evacuated areas and launched rocket attacks from distance. Basra Palace where UK forces were stationed was targeted, prompting the withdrawal of FCO civilian staff. The British commanders criticised the decision, arguing it undercut reconstruction, training and policing efforts. It seemed to confirm existing US suspicions that the British were operating unilaterally and without providing their coalition partners with due consultation. Moreover, it seemed to embolden the militias who saw the withdrawal as a sign of the success of their actions. By the end of November, Shirreff was complaining of resource shortages and the need to reduce the levels of indirect fire on the city. Politically, there was deep uncertainty created by the US midterm elections. The declining security situation had turned US public opinion against the war and the elections led to the Democrats gaining the Senate and House of Representatives. Uncertainty flourished in London over what effects this would have on coalition strategy in Iraq. In the meantime, the UK's policy hinged upon the 'successful' conclusion of Operation *Sinbad* and draw down of forces from 7,100 to 4,500 in May 2007. On the ground, any tactical successes were undermined by the militias moving back into areas once the troops had moved out. Elements of the ISF proved unreliable and the JAM were now vying with other smaller, but professional, militias for control in Basra. By January 2007, Blair was receiving mixed reports on the situation inside the city. Sir Nigel Sheinwald reported to the Prime Minister that the MOD were 'putting a positive gloss on Operation *Sinbad* because they are desperate to get down to 4,500 by May/June for Afghan reasons' (Chilcot et al., *Report of the Iraq Inquiry*, Vol. 8, p.71). At the end of January, a report was circulated among the government departments painting a picture of the insecurity faced by the people of Basra. As the operation reached its conclusion, its effects were ambiguous. In some areas, security and economic provisions had improved and the reputation of the MND (SE) rose, but the militia's influence remained wide ranging and pernicious.

Shirreff cut an isolated figure by the end of his tour in mid-January 2007; the FCO and DFID had taken his criticisms of civilian–military coordination of reconstruction badly, while the Permanent Joint Headquarters (PJHQ) was seeking a solution that would free resources for the Afghan theatre. Shirreff's end of tour report reaffirmed the importance of success in Iraq but noted the marginal line between success and failure. More tellingly, the report recognised the disparity between the theory of the UK's 'comprehensive approach' and the realities on the ground, which were frequently complicated by Whitehall's 'parsimony'. Shirreff was replaced by Major-General Jonathan Shaw and the new commander brought a fresh approach: one that would prove decidedly controversial.

Shaw planned to pivot MND (SE) away from primarily focusing on establishing security in Basra towards finding a political resolution with the principal opposing militia – the JAM. The situation, Shaw argued, was 'Palermo not Beirut' (Fairweather, *A War of Choice*, p.305). Yet simultaneously Shaw's options were being reduced. By January, the MOD was discussing a May withdrawal to Basra airport and a drawdown of 7,000 troops to 4,500. This would effectively cede control of Basra Palace and the downtown area to ISF control. Although the plan was later delayed until the summer, the problem remained unchanged: the ISF simply did not have the manpower, resources or command the loyalty to fill the void effectively. This also marked a significant breach with their US allies who were conducting an operational pivot of their own. After the disappointment of the November 2006 midterm elections, President Bush replaced Secretary of State Donald Rumsfeld with Robert Gates. The latter had been part of the Iraq Study Group (ISG) and was a proponent of a greater US commitment of ground forces.

By the end of January 2007, General Casey and US Ambassador to Iraq, Zalmay Khalilzad, were showing concerns about the UK's plans to withdraw from Basra Palace. Downing Street clung to the successes of Operation *Sinbad*, the ISF presence and the relative stability of the area. But, as Dominic Asquith, the British ambassador

On 10 January 2007, President George W. Bush announced that he would be deploying 20,000 more US service personnel to support the Iraqi government in its efforts to pacify the inflamed sectarian conflict. The '**Surge**' was announced in the face of fierce domestic and international criticism but enabled the US to expand their training and stabilisation operations. It coincided with a time when moderate Sunni opinion was beginning to turn against hard-line Islamism, prompting what is now known as the '**Anbar Awakening**'. This was the forming of a Sunni tribal coalition supported by the US to combat radicalism in Al-Anbar Province. Taken together, these two changes provided the military strength and political will to reduce violence across Iraq in 2007 and 2008.

to Iraq reported to the FCO, there was a strong view amongst key US figures that the UK would 'continue to make the facts fit our timelines' (Chilcot et al., *Report of the Iraq Inquiry*, Vol. 8, p.91). The pressure of the new, ferocious campaign underway in Helmand Province, Afghanistan, placed competing demands for equipment and manpower that simply could not be met concurrently with an expanded or even ongoing commitment to Iraq. So, while the UK was busy preparing to fold its hand, the US was about to go all-in.

At the heart of Britain's new strategy was an attempt to find the reconcilable elements within the JAM. If Major-General Shaw could reach an accommodation to bring the principal Shia militia into the new Iraqi political system, he might reduce the violence aimed at British forces and within Basra itself. Talks probably began in late 2006 with Ahmed al-Fartosi; the captured hard-line militia leader who had previously caused the British in Basra so many problems in 2004. By June 2007, an agreement steadily took shape. First, a trial ceasefire was scheduled for 15–17 June. To secure this, coalition forces would agree to stop targeting JAM cells and release two militia detainees. If this was successful, a longer period with more releases would follow. Unbeknownst to Fartosi, those prisoners pencilled in for release were already scheduled to be freed that month. The initial ceasefire markedly reduced the indirect fire targeted at the Basra Palace and further plans to build trust between the British and Fartosi's militia took form. Two further detainees would be released (classified as 'some threat to coalition forces') and strike operations against the JAM would cease, except in self-defence and to interdict weapons or at the behest of the Iraqi government. In return, all indirect-fire attacks on the coalition's Basra Palace headquarters would cease. Throughout July, plans for the ceasefire developed but they faced impediments. There was reluctance within the British political and military establishment over the unreliability of Fartosi and what the JAM were getting out of the deal. Over July, the pressure mounted to expand the geographic area of the ceasefire and the type of attacks that were included. While the Secret Intelligence Service (SIS but commonly known as MI6) negotiated with Fartosi, apprehension was building over the US response. Efforts to present the deal as akin to those struck by the US were rebuffed given the improvements the surge had brought about in Baghdad. The Iraqi Prime Minister Nouri al-Maliki was also deeply unconvinced, despite his previous unwillingness for the British to clamp down on the JAM during Operation *Sinbad*. Shia support had shifted once more leading to a fracture between the Sadrists and Maliki. The Iraqi Prime Minister now favoured more resolute action.

The critical factor that tilted the balance was the resignation of Tony Blair and Gordon Brown's ascension to the role of British Prime Minister which occurred on 27 June 2007. Brown was determined to cut the Gordian knot of British involvement in Iraq and, although outwardly committed, he pushed for a quick withdrawal from Basra Palace, leading to a short period in 'overwatch' at Basra airport. The withdrawal of British personnel from downtown Basra was scheduled for the end of August. The ceasefire deal was soon seen as the best way for the British to extract themselves peacefully. It was hoped that the withdrawal and the transition of the JAM to political power might pacify the area. When the accommodation with the Sadrist militia came into effect on 13 August 2007, all attacks effectively stopped. On 3 September 2007, the last British soldiers left Basra Palace and relocated to the airport and Shaibah logistics base on the outskirts of the city. The truce held and Basra outwardly seemed peaceful. Britain's extreme pragmatism had seemed to work. But scratch the surface and the JAM's rule was one of brutality. Despite the token Iraqi Army presence, General Mohan al-Furayji did not have the force to quell the militias; kidnappings, rape and murder went unchecked for four months. As long as the British had prisoners to release, they were left in peace, but on 31 December 2007, the final prisoner, Ahmed Fartosi himself, was freed. Days later, the attacks restarted.

By early February 2008, a small British team, including Colonel Richard Iron and RMAS academic and counterinsurgency expert Daniel Marston, began briefing senior figures on the realities of the insurgency raging on the streets of Basra. Iron coordinated with General Mohan al-Furayji to lay down the outlines of an Iraqi-led operation to retake the city. The key to the new plan was gaining the support of both Prime Minister Maliki and the new head of US operations, General David Petraeus. Over the course of March, a series of briefings paved the way for what would become Operation *Charge of the Knights*. On 24 March, Maliki moved to the city to oversee the operation personally.

When the Iraqi 10th and 14th Divisions began moving against militia positions on 25 March 2008, the US and UK were completely wrong-footed. The limited flow of information from senior Iraqi figures left the coalition unable to provide anything other than the most rudimentary logistics support. The first days of the operation went predictably badly, with ISF underestimating the resolve and tactical nous of their opponents. The US and British scrambled to respond. By 28 March, US and UK air power began to support the ISF more proactively. Nonetheless, by 30 March, the situation changed decisively when the Iranians backed a cease fire between Moqtada al Sadr's militia forces and the Iraqi government. On 31 March, the JAM stood down, their leader – under Iranian pressure – had turned decisively towards a political resolution. Operations against hardliners continued into April, with US and British support, and the city was effectively back under Maliki's control. As *Charge of the Knights* concluded, British efforts returned once more to 'overwatch' and reconstruction. Troop numbers held at 4,100 until the bulk of the British contingent was withdrawn in June 2009. The US remained in greater numbers into 2011.

The profound differences of approach between the British and United States in responding to the increased violence in Iraq were a result of the different political pressures. While public opinion had turned against the war in both countries, the British saw their presence as a cause for violence. The US, on the other hand, viewed security as a necessary precursor to withdrawal and were willing to commit extra personnel and resources to achieve that. British policy looked to pressure Iraq's key politicians to face up to the responsibilities of securing their own cities by handing over to provincial control as soon as possible. In this, key figures like Maliki conspired to undermine their efforts, either curtailing British operations such as *Sinbad* or limiting their operational freedom by demanding restrictive rules of engagement. While Basra remained comparatively placid, the effects of this divergence could be explained away, but as the violence rose, the fractures became more noticeable. The accommodation with Fartosi and al-Sadr's militia was borne of a desire for the UK to withdraw from the country and reduce attacks on British personnel. But in doing so they ceded control of Basra to their enemies. The US may well have been guilty of acting out of blind principle in the first post-invasion years, but here was an incidence of the British acting too pragmatically. What seemed like political compromise to the deal makers looked suspiciously like capitulation to the Americans and Iraqis. The effects of this were devastating in the short term. Crime spiked and the ISF proved incapable of asserting its authority. In the medium term, Maliki was forced to confront the challenge to his authority in southern Iraq but at the cost of enormous reputational damage for the British whom he blamed for letting the situation get to this stage. Many senior US figures saw the chaotic scramble of Operation *Charge of the Knights* as a direct result of British bungling. Ultimately, the UK tried to play the role of the dutiful ally, while attempting to sneak out of the back door.

From 2006 onwards, it became clear that Britain's approach required a complete rethink. The US had undergone something similar before General David Petraeus's deployment in January 2007. Building upon 'clear, hold, build', the US Counterinsurgency Center produced a new US Army and Marine Corps doctrine promoting principles geared around protecting and winning over the people. FM 3-24 was published in December 2006, but it was the product of a considered assessment of the current state of Iraq and relevant past examples. The process of this new doctrine's adoption is well described in Peter Mansoor's *Surge* (2014). Petraeus oversaw multiple revisions and coordinated expert input. His position first within MNSTC-I, later as head of the Counterinsurgency Center and finally as the commander of MNF-I allowed him to disseminate the new approach widely. FM 3-24 enshrined the United States' new approach; the objective was establishing legitimate government, which required a unified effort between the military and civil components. Political consideration must come before immediate tactical necessity and operations that did not consider the political effects would likely have unintended or detrimental consequences. As the environment (terrain, politics, economics and society) could profoundly shape any counterinsurgency campaign, reliable intelligence must be the driver for operations. Moving on, the manual noted that insurgents had to be isolated from their support to be defeated. The counterinsurgent force must then provide security and uphold the rule of law and, to do so, must prepare over the long term. These broad principles were then buttressed by more specific advice on a range of matters, such as intelligence, campaign design and the development of 'host-nation security forces'.

While FM 3-24 brought a slow adjustment to the US conduct of counterinsurgency operations, it did not transform the situation overnight. The coalition's forces faced different opposition in different regions and approached their operations with different mindsets shaped by nationality and circumstance. The British were no more immune to these difficulties than any other nation and it would take more than three years for their doctrine to be comprehensively updated. The US used FM 3-24 to standardise and update their approach to counterinsurgency. The British, however, combined post-tour reports and organic adaptation to effect change. Although the UK's main doctrinal manual was updated in 2007 to reflect the new operational challenges, it was, for all intents and purposes, a minor update to the 2001 *AFM 1-10: Counter Insurgency Operations*. When the British finally came to write *AFM 1-10: Countering Insurgency* (2009), it captured the changes in approach that had evolved out of their experiences in Iraq and Afghanistan.

Afghanistan and the Birth of Modern British Counterinsurgency

In May 2006, the first British Brigade (16 Air Assault) was deployed, in half strength, to Helmand province as part of the International Security Assistance Force (ISAF). Despite two planning teams being sent ahead in 2005 to assess the likely threats and resistance to the British deployment, the strength of the Taliban was dramatically underestimated. The resultant Joint Helmand Plan's advice stressed the uncertainty of opposition in the province and recommended that Britain's small force concentrate on securing the key towns of Lashkar Gah and Gereshk. Nonetheless, as Theo Farrell has observed, these warnings became secondary to political necessities. Senior figures felt that Britain needed to deploy troops in early 2006 to recover some of the prestige lost by the descent of Basra into militia control (Farrell, *Unwinnable,* pp.145–151). Consequently, advice suggesting that British policymakers and operatives attempt to form a deeper understanding of Helmand before forces were deployed was ignored. The 'oil-spot' strategy of using British troops to secure the towns was adopted but greatly expanded at the behest of Mohammed Daoud, the new governor. This pushed the few combat troops into isolated 'platoon houses' of 40–100 men across the province. Rather than the two major urban centres, the British also had to garrison positions in Now Zad, Sangin, Kajaki and Musa Qala. To make matters worse, the recently removed, corrupt, governor, Sher Mohammed Akhundzada, swung his militia of 3,000 men across to the Taliban. For the next six months, the isolated garrisons came under constant insurgent attack.

The Taliban's tactics were often unsophisticated but determined. They kept the platoon houses under near constant small-arms and RPG fire. Detachments of 3 Battalion Parachute Regiment (3 Para) became effectively isolated in Sangin and Musa Qala, and they relied upon aerial resupply which stretched the limits of the few available Chinook helicopters. By July, a further 800 troops were deployed to Helmand but the situation remained precarious. The platoon houses relied upon heavy firepower to defend themselves. Far from protecting the people, the stretched British troops were causing devastation in the areas they garrisoned. Apache helicopter gunships and the American A-10 Warthogs proved lethal against insurgents but also flattened huge sections of the towns they were there to protect. Musa Qala was torn to pieces. The paratroopers were not shy about using their own organic firepower either. Javelin missiles were effective against entrenched insurgent fire positions but destroyed whole sections of civilian compounds, which otherwise might have housed locals. By September 2006, British forces had decided to withdraw from Musa Qala. An agreement was reached at the prompting of the area's tribal elders for the Taliban and, later, the British to withdraw from the town. A local *Loya Jirga* (grand assembly) was appointed to oversee reconstruction and would act as an extension of the Afghan government. The 'Musa Qala accord', as it came to be known, allowed the British to withdraw, but it had opponents in the Afghan government and among the US forces. It stood little chance of holding. By late January, the local Taliban leader exacted revenge for a US airstrike that killed his brother by marching into Musa Qala and dismantling the *Loya Jirga*. He was killed in early February 2007, but the deal was over. 16 Air Assault Brigade's first tour of Helmand was intense. Battling against a

Sangin was a key location and saw much military action.

determined opponent and under-resourced, the soldiers clung on in dangerously exposed positions. But after six months the Taliban tacitly recognised their need to regroup and recover. Ceasefires in Now Zad and Sangin were agreed with varying degrees of success. The ceasefire in Now Zad collapsed in a matter of weeks, but Sangin held until March 2007. This would change the conditions for the incoming 3 Commando Brigade who shifted operational approach when they took over in October 2006.

3 Commando Brigade recognised the static character of the fighting that had taken place during 16 Air Assault Brigade's tour and wanted to reassert ISAF's freedom of manoeuvre within Helmand province. Rather than relying on the fixed presence of British troops in urban centres to tackle the Taliban, Brigadier Jerry Thomas, commanding the task force, established Mobile Operations Groups (MOGs) of 250 men in 40 light vehicles who would sally forth to find and attack the enemy. In principle, the plan had merits. It should have restored the ability of British forces to engage their opponents on their terms and minimise the damage to the towns. The brigade recognised the importance of influencing the population and started out with the intention of avoiding escalation. In reality, the Taliban proved capable of evading 3 Commando Brigade's attempts to draw them into unfavourable battles and frequently drew the British into ambushes of their own. As Farrell has noted, this became known to the Royal Marines, who formed the bulk of the force, as 'advancing to ambush'. The long-range sweeps and ceasefires in Musa Qala and Sangin reduced the pressure on British bases elsewhere in Helmand, but they failed to de-escalate the insurgency. Pitched battles were fought in Kajaki, Now Zad, Garmsir and Sangin, leaving further devastation in their wake. The next brigade in the six-month rotation were no less able to dampen the violence that was raging in Helmand.

12 Mechanised Brigade refocused the campaign on the Afghan Development Zone (ADZ). This was the centre of economic and political life in Helmand province. The previous brigades had recognised the importance of the ADZ that centred around Gereshk

and Lashkar Gah but extended their protection of it northwards along the Sangin valley to Sangin itself. However, in being drawn into actions in the north and long-range strike operations, there was little in the way of development in the ADZ. 12 Mechanised Brigade intended to change that by adopting a defensive posture elsewhere in Helmand. Operations were launched to clear the Sangin valley of Taliban and establish bases to control the territory. By the end of the tour, 12 Mechanised Brigade had been involved in 1,096 major engagements and fired nearly 2.5 million rounds of ammunition, more than the previous two brigades combined. Reconstruction efforts were ponderous. Local politics and corruption undermined infrastructure improvement and the Afghan National Army (ANA) was still too underdeveloped to be able to hold the ground captured. The Afghan National Police (ANP) were expected to fill the gap and provide a permanent presence, but they proved corrupt and unreliable. The plan to control the terrain and deny the Taliban freedom to move amongst the population in a key area of Helmand province was well conceived but poorly executed. Without larger troop numbers and resources, it was impossible for ISAF to bolster the legitimacy and authority of Hamid Karzai's regime.

The first three British brigade rotations (Operations *Herrick IV*, *V* and *VI*) had all employed different operational strategies. The fourth deployment, 52 Brigade on Operation *Herrick VII*, would change it once again. This time, however, they would adopt methods and principles that would form the foundations of the British effort moving forward. Rather than focusing on territory, like the ADZ, a population-centric approach was adopted. This involved securing and persuading the Helmand people to support ISAF or at least withdraw support from the Taliban. The publication of the US FM 3-24 provided a loose framework for Brigadier Andrew Mackay's 52 Brigade. In practice, this meant troops being stationed in Forward Operating Bases (FOBs) for the entire tour to enhance their understanding of local patterns of behaviour and offer security. Influence operations gained increased resources; and new measures of assessment were introduced to gauge Afghan public opinion and improve ISAF's reconstruction efforts. This resulted in the Tactical Conflict Assessment Framework (TCAF). It was supplemented by Non-Kinetic Effects Teams (N-KETS) who were stationed at battle-group headquarters. They were tasked with planning non-violent operations to alter Afghan public opinion and swing local support towards ISAF. Additionally, towards the end of *Herrick VII*, the UK's civilian-led Provincial Reconstruction Team (PRT) was bolstered with additional resources, manpower and leadership. This expanded further during 16 Air Assault Brigade's second tour (*Herrick VIII*), effectively tripling the size from just under 50 to 142 civilian and military personnel. The British brigades made a concerted attempt to de-escalate levels of violence. Musa Qala was recaptured after efforts were made to dissuade local Taliban commanders from getting involved. On 7/8 December 2007, the US Task Force Fury swept through the town supported by British and American airpower firing precision munitions. The Taliban resistance collapsed rapidly and within days civilians forced out by the fighting began to return. Local optimism swiftly turned to disappointment as reconciliation efforts were undermined by Afghan officials who saw little opportunity to enrich themselves through the project.

The change in counterinsurgent approach coincided with a shift in the Taliban's methods. Throughout 2008, they moved away from frequent, direct confrontation in firefights with ISAF troops towards more calculated attacks coupled with a major expansion in the use of IEDs. One such planned attack took place on 10 October 2008 when approximately 300 Taliban moved to attack Lashkar Gah. British and US airpower swiftly annihilated the insurgents causing 150 casualties of which 50 per cent were killed. The attack was traced back to Nad-e-Ali which, along with Marjah, had steadily been infiltrated by Taliban since 2007. On 7 December 2008, Operation *Sond Chara* was launched to clear the Nad-e-Ali area. In cold and wet conditions, British, Danish and Estonian troops swept the area and successfully restored a moderate level of control. Soon, however,

IEDs greatly curtailed ISAF's freedom of movement. The next two tours in 2009 and 2010 by 19 Light Brigade and 11 Brigade led to two more major operations to clear the insurgent threat from Lashkar Gah. Operation *Panchai Palang* (or Operation *Panther's Claw* in English) began in June 2009 and involved 3,000 ISAF troops clearing the 'Babaji Pear' in northern Nad-e-Ali. ISAF planners had realised throughout 2007 and 2008 that civilian casualties were fanning the flames of insurgency. Consequently, to avoid antagonising the local population, *Panchai Palang* was preceded by clear indications that the attack was coming. This warning helped civilians move away from the area and encouraged insurgents to flee rather than fight. These methods were then replicated in December 2009's Operation *Tor Shpah* and February 2010's Operation *Moshtarak*. These final two operations were coupled with local negotiations with tribal elders to add pressure to the Taliban to avoid confrontation. Despite the messaging, IEDs took a heavy toll on the units involved. The commanding officer of the Welsh Guards, Lieutenant Colonel Rupert Thorneloe, was killed when his Viking armoured vehicle was hit by an IED during *Panchai Palang*. 19 Light Brigade's tour incurred 406 casualties of which 78 were killed, the vast majority by IED.

A number of factors helped ISAF and the British Task Force Helmand address the weaknesses of earlier operations. The most immediate was the decision taken in 2009 to deploy the US 2nd Marine Expeditionary Brigade. These extra troops freed the British to concentrate on the later operations. In December 2009, President Barack Obama declared that 30,000 more US soldiers were being deployed to Afghanistan. This influx followed a reorganisation of ISAF leadership structures that brought General Stanley McChrystal to Afghanistan as commander and the establishment of ISAF Joint Command (IJC) to oversee a unified campaign strategy. McChrystal saw the problem of Afghanistan in broadly the same manner as the British brigades had done from *Herrick VII* onwards. The counterinsurgent strategy supported the population-centric approach, although it was now supplemented with a much larger programme to kill or capture the Taliban's commanders using US special operations forces. Regular US forces would be used to establish a permanent presence in places where ISAF's grip was weak. Progressively, the US Marines took over most of north and southern Helmand province, allowing the British to focus on the centre of the region. Nevertheless, on the ground, the conduct between the two allies varied markedly. The US Marines developed a reputation for ferocity, and as the Taliban tactics shifted away from direct confrontation and towards IEDs, the Marines took no chances destroying any compounds or structures that seemed to pose a threat. Bold action by the US Marines had pacified much of the Upper Sangin Valley but this came at the cost of their relationship with the local populace who saw little tangible benefit from the fighting that had raged across the region since 2006.

On 23 June 2010, General Stanley McChrystal was removed from his post and replaced by General David Petraeus. McChrystal had previously given an impolitic interview to a *Rolling Stone* journalist criticising Vice-President Joe Biden and was seen by Obama as agitating against the civilian leadership. A new commander brought yet another new strategy. Petraeus expanded McChrystal's kill/ capture programme, which targeted middle-ranking Taliban leaders. It was hoped that wiping out the operational command structure of the opposition would fracture the insurgency. Despite over 2,000 Taliban operatives, of which 285 were insurgent leaders, being killed or taken prisoner from July–September 2010, the policy failed to undermine the Taliban's capacity to target ISAF and Afghan troops. The programme served only to undermine the unity between the US, UK and Afghan governments. By the summer of 2010, there was a ticking clock on the Afghan campaign. Public support for the ongoing war was falling to between 30–40 per cent in most Western European nations and Canada. Obama aimed to begin withdrawing surge troops by March 2011. The new British Prime Minister, David Cameron, consulted with civilian, political and military experts and concluded that the withdrawal of British forces should begin before the next general election in 2015. When Hamid Karzai set out his vision of the transition to Afghan responsibility before December 2014, the date was set. More resources were funnelled into training programmes for the Afghan security forces. Significant attacks continued to occur such as the Taliban's assault on Camp Bastion in September 2012, but the most significant new threat emerged from 'green-on-blue' or 'green-on-green' attacks, whereby Afghans turned their weapons on Western soldiers or their fellow Afghans. The reasons for these attacks varied and not all attacks were coordinated by the Taliban, but it prompted ISAF to look carefully at the vetting process.

On 28 October 2014, Camp Bastion was handed over the ANA and the last British combat troops were withdrawn from Afghanistan. The war has not stopped for the Afghans though, and the fall of Kunduz and large swathes of the country to Taliban control shows there is still much hard fighting ahead. For the British, the conditions faced between 2006 and 2010 in Afghanistan and Iraq shaped the adoption of new principles of counterinsurgency. Yet unlike the Americans who more methodically standardised and formulated

---

Ten Principles of Counterinsurgency

Primacy of political purpose
Unity of effort
Understand the human terrain
Secure the population
Neutralise the insurgent
Gain and maintain popular support
Operate in accordance with the law
Integrate Intelligence
Prepare for the long term
Learn and adapt

(*AFM 1-10: Countering Insurgency*)

their approach throughout 2006 and attempted to coordinate it with changing national policy, the British adapted in a more ad hoc fashion. Change was driven at the brigade level and the adoption of a new doctrine for counterinsurgency followed practice rather than shaping it in the first instance. Later *AFM 1-10: Countering Insurgency* would support the principles that guided the UK's conduct in Afghanistan. The ten principles laid out in the manual built upon Britain's extensive history of colonial policing and managing the process of decolonisation. The legacy of Charles Gwynn, Robert Thompson and Frank Kitson can be traced through the emphasis on managing intelligence, securing the population and acting in accordance with the law. These ideas were updated, supplemented and applied to the modern operational environment. They remain the bedrock of the British army's approach to counterinsurgency.

Yet despite the doctrinal recognition of the primacy and importance of politics, it was in the political sphere where NATO failed so comprehensively. Afghanistan has certainly seen some improvements, particularly for the lives of women in the more secure areas, but the inability of the US and UK to master the complex web of loyalties in Afghanistan fundamentally undermined the efforts to pacify and defeat the Taliban. Corruption permeated all levels of Karzai's regime, while Pakistan proved to be a fickle ally; unable to master the divisions cutting through its own society and frequently harbouring divided loyalties. This was brought sharply into the public eye when Osama Bin Laden was killed by US Special Forces on 2 May 2011 in Abbottabad, Pakistan. While British and US doctrines both stress the need for political resolutions, they have proven rather more elusive to reach in practice. In both Iraq and Afghanistan, the US and UK were tethered to regimes that often lacked widespread legitimacy. As Mike Martin has noted in *An Intimate War* (2014), this was further complicated by the factional nature of Afghan politics. Loyalties to the Karzai regime and the Taliban were often reinforced by local allegiances and tribal divisions. While the British doctrine recognised the difficulties of handling the complex 'human terrain', in reality it was more difficult to acquire. ISAF frequently lacked a full understanding or the bureaucratic flexibility to respond to local factors when they did have a grasp. Over the course of the war in Afghanistan, British training in Afghan culture improved markedly but there was no overcoming the fact that they were outsiders to the country, and they came with a long and troubled history of colonial conquest.

Conclusion

The wars in Iraq and Afghanistan created a surge in interest in counterinsurgency and its practice. Doctrine was updated, and a flood of books published on campaigns past and present. The manuals produced remain the bedrock of the UK and USA's approach to insurgent warfare. The lessons of Gwynn, Galula and Thompson once more became relevant, but the difficult experiences of the coalition forces in Iraq sharpened the need for an updated set of principles. Thus, new experiences merged with classical ideas to create a further evolution in military thinking on counterinsurgency. The US and UK differed in the way they addressed these problems and national politics has, at moments, undermined the relationship. Both, however, have reached a rough consensus on adhering to a population-centric approach to counterinsurgency. These principles form a handrail that might guide future conduct without prescribing any ill-fitting solution. And, ultimately, as the character of insurgency changes so must the principles of counterinsurgency.

The outcome of the last two of what have been collectively termed as 'Blair's Wars' still remains controversial and ambiguous. Iraq and Afghanistan today are still two of the most unstable countries in the world. Continued conflict, corruption and instability left Iraq 137th and Afghanistan 162nd out of 166 countries on the Legatum Prosperity Index in 2020. The rapidly changing strategic situation complicates any judgements historians might make. It is inevitable that as the long-term consequences of the wars begin to unfold judgements might change. Later scholars will have more material and a clearer view from which to assess the events that took place. The recency of the two campaigns has frequently blurred the lines between participant and objective observer. Many accounts, excellent though they are, draw heavily upon personal experiences or close observation. The frequent danger of this for the historian is a narrowness of viewpoint or limitation of experience, but the diversity and range of accounts from both conflicts helps to offset this to a significant degree. Nevertheless, the reader should be aware that the conclusions regarding the war remain highly contentious and will invariably change in future.

Conclusion

This book has not sought to provide a comprehensive history of counterinsurgency. Instead, by examining a range of case studies, it has identified several themes for consideration. First, there are numerous difficulties involved in defining key terms. Second, the diversity of the case studies examined here raises the question of whether it is possible to speak of general principles of counterinsurgency that can be applied in all contexts. Instead, it is clear that some principles required modification. However, it is also clear that some common ideas did develop, for example through the influential writings of Thompson, Galula and others, and through the emergence of the study of counterinsurgency as a subject in its own right. Third, the gap between theory and practice has been made apparent throughout. Fourth, the book considered the extent to which counterinsurgency is about coercion or 'winning hearts and minds'. Fifth, it stressed the importance of key factors on both sides, such as external support for the insurgents and developing a plausible cause for the counterinsurgents. Sixth, counterinsurgency campaigns provided complex environments, in which it was necessary to innovate and adapt. Finally, it is important to examine the challenges posed by insurgencies today in their proper historical context.

As the British Army's Field Manual *Countering Insurgency* (2010) makes clear, 'Counterinsurgency is warfare'. Writers on all sides, from Mao to Thompson, have noted that it is political, but also that it involves violence; as Kitson observed, it is violence that distinguishes insurgency from mere disorder. However, defining counterinsurgency is difficult because counterinsurgency, like unconventional or irregular warfare, is defined by its opposite. As we have seen, Callwell recognised the weaknesses of his definition that small wars included 'all campaigns other than those where both the opposing sides consist of regular troops' (Callwell, *Small Wars*, p.21). The usefulness of the term, therefore, depended on his interpretation of what 'regular' warfare was (to him, the European warfare of his time), and perhaps more importantly, it covered everything under the sun that was not 'regular'. Colin S. Gray dealt with this issue in his 2007 article, 'Irregular Warfare: One Nature, Many Characters'. He raised an important question. 'Irregularity is defined by its opposite,' he argued. 'This is not terribly helpful. It tells us that irregular warfare is not regular warfare. But what is regular warfare? And to whom?' (p.43). What about regular forces which act 'irregularly', in other words outside the norms of European warfare? This could certainly be said to have happened in colonial campaigns. The term 'small war' is a Eurocentric term suggestive of a war of lesser importance, a conflict on the periphery, where European armies could get away with much more than they could in what they called 'civilised' warfare. In order to understand the term counterinsurgency, then, it is crucial to understand the insurgency that is being countered, in order to develop an appropriate response. This was easier said than done, and more often than not the history of counterinsurgency is the story of the failure to understand.

However, counterinsurgents were able to fall back on a set of increasingly common principles, something of a counterinsurgency canon. Many of these principles were established in the context of colonial warfare. The 'sideways spread of influence' from one country to another can be seen in Callwell's use of examples drawn from the colonial campaigns of other countries and, at a practical level, in the use of concentration camps in Cuba, the Philippines and South Africa. Whereas colonial wars were limited in terms of ends and means for the imperial power, they often tended towards greater totality for their opponents. That remained the case in the 20th century. The Vietnam War was more total for the US's opponents, or indeed for the RVN, than it was for the USA. The Algerian War was not a total war for France, in spite of the rhetoric of *guerre révolutionnaire*. Moreover, the methods developed in the 19th century proved remarkably durable. The sweeps and drives of the South African War were not so different to the cordon and sweep operations in Malaya and Kenya. Air policing substituted the use of new technology, in the form of aircraft, for the traditional punitive expedition.

One of the major themes running through the book was the close, but frequently uneasy, relationship between counterinsurgency in theory and counterinsurgency in practice. The ideas that have shaped insurgency and counterinsurgency have frequently smoothed over the difficult realities of these campaigns. What worked in one campaign did not necessarily work in another. Simson perhaps came up with the best analogy to describe the gap between theory and practice: it was like 'the difference between reading and seeing a play' (Simson, *British Rule, and Rebellion*, p.131). Mao's influence on counterinsurgency thinking also proved a mixed bag. Galula believed that counterinsurgents needed sound theory to work from because Mao had theorised the other side, and Westmoreland kept a copy of Mao beside his bed, but the positive outcomes of all of this are less clear.

Another major issue is the level of violence used in counterinsurgency. The relationship between carrot and stick, between coercion and 'hearts and minds', is best seen as a spectrum, rather than an either/or. As the scholarship of historians like David French and Karl Hack has shown, even the counterinsurgency that is seen as the archetypal 'hearts and minds' effort, the British campaign in the Malayan Emergency, involved significant use of coercion. At the same time, the British fought a 'dirty war' in Kenya that involved an even greater extent of coercion, calling into question the idea of a 'British way' in counterinsurgency. At the very least, exemplary force needs to be returned to the story. The conflicts in Cyprus and Northern Ireland were different because of their European setting (indeed UK setting in the latter case), but even here coercion featured heavily. The same tensions are readily visible in the other examples explored in this book. The Algerian War and the Vietnam War both involved a 'hearts and minds' element, but coercion played a major or, indeed, a greater role. It is also important to bear in mind the civil war aspect in insurgency, which is often underrated. In imperial wars of conquest, and then of decolonisation, large numbers of indigenous troops and police stood behind the European 'thin white line'. Daniel Branch focused on the extent to which the violence in the emergency in Kenya forced people to choose sides, and the same process is clear in the other case studies here, be it the increasing radicalisation of the settler leaders in Algeria, or the effect sectarian conflict had in Iraq.

External support is often a critical factor in deciding the outcome of a campaign. Many of the examples used in this book involved some degree of external support. Galula saw outside help as potentially essential to the success of the insurgent cause, and in practice, the British success in Malaya compared to US failure in Vietnam had much to do with the degree of external support for the insurgency in the latter case, rather than some in-built superiority in counterinsurgency that the British possessed. The examples of the Algerian War and the emergency in Cyprus both demonstrate the importance of the international arena: wars can be won and lost at least in part because of success or failure on the diplomatic front. Home fronts also matter: if insurgents start with a cause and counterinsurgents do not, the latter needs to find one or otherwise risk its people and soldiers questioning what they are fighting for.

The reciprocal nature of war is clearly visible in the action/reaction dynamic in insurgency and counterinsurgency, as the contending sides innovated, learned and responded to the activities of their opponent. This dynamic is clearly visible throughout the case studies explored here. In the end, the US lost its war in Vietnam not because it failed to learn or to 'do counterinsurgency properly'; instead, it lost in spite of its efforts to forge an effective strategy and not because that effort was lacking at all.

A final theme relates to contemporary insurgency. First, to what extent are the works of Galula, Trinquier, Thompson and Kitson still relevant today? As Jonathan Gumz has written, 'we have to avoid using history as a bland cupboard from which to raid lessons learned which serve to confirm ideas already arrived at in the present' (Gumz, 'Reframing the Historical Problematic of Insurgency', p.581). Some of the principles established by these authors may still apply, others will not and others still will apply with modifications. Simplistic narratives will not do, such as the idea that counterinsurgency is inherently more complex than conventional warfare or that 'lessons learned' offer a panacea for all ills. The surge in interest in counterinsurgency during the wars in Afghanistan and Iraq led to many important developments. The US and British armies wrote new counterinsurgency manuals. There was a renewed focus on how to 'do' counterinsurgency, followed by the emergence of a more critical narrative that questioned whether counterinsurgency was really about hearts and minds, and whether it was even a separate category of warfare at all. The time is now ripe for more historical analysis of what happened in Afghanistan and Iraq, and why.

Select Bibliography

Primary

Manuals and Reports

Australian Army, *Land Warfare Doctrine LWD 3-0-1 Counterinsurgency* (Canberra: Australian Defence Organisation, 2009) Chapter 1-1

British Army, *Army Field Manual (AFM) Vol.1 Combined Arms Operations Part 10: Counter Insurgency Operations (Strategic and Operational Guidelines)* (London: MOD, 2001)

British Army, *AFM Vol.1 Combined Arms Operations Part 10: Counter Insurgency Operations (Strategic and Operational Guidelines) Revised and Updated Version* (London: MOD, 2007)

British Army, *AFM Vol.1 Part 10: Countering Insurgency* (London: MOD, 2009, updated Jan 2010)

British Government, *Report of the Bloody Sunday Inquiry* (2010)

British Government, Chilcot et al., *Report of the Iraq Inquiry* (2016)

European Court of Human Rights, The Republic of Ireland v. The United Kingdom, http://lawofwar.org/Ireland_v_United_Kingdom.htm (1978)

General Orders No. 100: The Lieber Code, https://avalon.law.yale.edu/19th_century/lieber.asp

US Army, *FM 31-16, Department of the Army Field Manual: Counterguerrilla Operations* (Department of the Army, 1963)

US Army, *The US Army and Marine Corps Army Field Manual 3-24: Counterinsurgency (FM 3-24)* (Washington DC: Department of the Army, 2007)

US Joint Chiefs, *Joint Publication 3-24 Counterinsurgency* (Washington DC: Department of Defense, 2018)

War Office, *Field Service Regulations Vol.1: Organization and Administration* (London: HMSO, 1930)

War Office, 'Notes on Imperial Policing' (1934), TNA WO 279/796

Theorists and Practitioners

Tom Barry, *Guerilla Days in Ireland* (Cork: Mercier Press, 2011 [1946])

Tony Blair, *A Journey* (London: Hutchinson, 2010)

L. Paul Bremer III, *My Year in Iraq* (New York: Threshold, 2006)

George W. Bush, *Selected Speeches of President George W. Bush,* https://georgew-bush-whitehouse.archives.gov/infocus/bushrecord/documents/Selected_Speeches_George_W_Bush.pdf

C. E. Callwell, *Small Wars: Their Principles and Practice* (Lincoln: University of Nebraska Press, 1996 [1906])

Michael Carver, *Out of Step: Memoirs of a Field Marshal* (London: Hutchinson, 1989)

Carl von Clausewitz, *Vom Kriege* (Bonn: Dümmler, 1832: Werner Halhweg edition 1991)

Nathaniel Fick, *One Bullet Away: the Making of a Marine Officer* (New York: Houghton Mifflin Harcourt, 2005).

David Galula, *Counterinsurgency Warfare: Theory and Practice* (Westport, CT: Praeger Security International, 2006 [1964])

Charles W. Gwynn, *Imperial Policing* (London: Macmillan, 1939 [1934])

Frank Kitson, *Gangs and Counter-Gangs* (London: Barne & Rockliff, 1960);

_____, *Low Intensity Operations: Subversion, Insurgency and Peacekeeping* (London: Faber & Faber, 2010 [1971])

_____, *Bunch of Five* (London: Faber & Faber, 2010 [1977])

_____, *Directing Operations* (London: Faber & Faber, 2011 [1989])

T.E. Lawrence, 'Twenty-Seven Articles', https://wwi.lib.byu.edu/index.php/The_27_Articles_of_T.E._Lawrence

Carlos Marighella, *The Minimanual of the Urban Guerrilla* (1969)

John J. McCuen, *The Art of Counter-Revolutionary War* (London: Faber, 1969 [1966])

Harold G. Moore and Joseph L. Galloway, *We Were Soldiers Once ... And Young* (London: Corgi, 2002 [1992])

H. J. Simson, *British Rule, and Rebellion* (Edinburgh: William Blackwood and Sons Ltd., 1937)

Robert Thompson, *Defeating Communist Insurgency: Experiences from Malaya and Vietnam* (London: Chatto & Windus, 1966)

_____, *No Exit from Vietnam* (New York: David McKay, 1969)

_____, *Make for the Hills* (London: Leo Cooper, 1989)

Roger Trinquier, *Modern Warfare: A French View of Counterinsurgency* (London: Pall Mall Press, 1964 [1961])

William Westmoreland, *A Soldier Reports* (New York: Doubleday, 1976)

Christiaan de Wet, *Three Years War* (London: Constable, 1902)

Garnet J. Wolseley, *The Soldier's Pocket Book for Field Service*, 5th edn (London: Macmillan, 1886)

Secondary

Books

David Anderson, *Histories of the Hanged: Britain's Dirty War in Kenya and the End of Empire* (London: Weidenfeld & Nicolson, 2005)

Simon Anglim, *Orde Wingate: Unconventional Warrior* (Barnsley: Pen and Sword, 2014)

Huw Bennett, *Fighting the Mau Mau: The British Army and Counter-Insurgency in the Kenya Emergency* (Cambridge: Cambridge University Press, 2012)

Daniel Branch, *Defeating Mau Mau, Creating Kenya: Counterinsurgency, Civil War, and Decolonization* (Cambridge: Cambridge University Press, 2009)

Peter Busch, *All the Way with JFK? Britain, the US, and the Vietnam War* (Oxford: Oxford University Press, 2003)

John Cloake, *Templer, Tiger of Malaya: the Life of Field Marshal Sir Gerald Templer* (London: Harrap, 1985)

Gregory A. Daddis, *Westmoreland's War: Reassessing American Strategy in Vietnam* (Oxford: Oxford University Press, 2014)

Caroline Elkins, *Britain's Gulag: The Brutal End of Empire in Kenya* (London: Pimlico, 2005)

Christopher Elliott, *High Command: British Military Leadership in the Iraq and Afghanistan Wars* (London: Hurst, 2015)

Richard English, *Armed Struggle: The History of the IRA* (London: Pan Macmillan, 2012 [2003]),

Richard English, *Terrorism: How to Respond* (Oxford: Oxford University Press, 2009)

Martin Evans, *Algeria: France's Undeclared War* (Oxford: Oxford University Press, 2012)

Jack Fairweather, *A War of Choice, Honour, Hubris and Sacrifice: The British in Iraq* (London: Vintage, 2012)

Theo Farrell, *Unwinnable: Britain's War in Afghanistan 2001-2014* (London: The Bodley Head, 2017)

Byron Farwell, *Queen Victoria's Little Wars* (London: Allen Lane, 1973)

Diarmaid Ferriter, *A Nation and Not a Rabble: The Irish Revolution 1913 -1923* (London: Profile, 2015)

Michael P. M. Finch, *A Progressive Occupation? The Gallieni-Lyautey Method and Colonial Pacification in Tonkin and Madagascar, 1885–1900* (Oxford: Oxford University Press, 2013)

David French, *The British Way in Counter-Insurgency, 1945–1967* (Oxford: Oxford University Press, 2011)

David French, *Fighting EOKA: The British Counter-Insurgency Campaign on Cyprus, 1955–1959* (Oxford: Oxford University Press, 2015)

John M. Gates, *Schoolbooks and Krags: The United States Army in the Philippines, 1899–1902* (Westport, CT: Greenwood Press, 1973)

Robert Gerwarth and John Horne (eds), *War in Peace: Paramilitary Violence in Europe After the Great War* (Oxford: Oxford University Press, 2012)

Antonio Giustozzi, *Koran, Kalashnikov and Laptop: The Neo-Taliban Insurgency in Afghanistan 2002–2007* (London: Hurst, 2007)

Michael Herr, *Dispatches* (London: Picador, 2015 [1977])

Michael Hopkinson, *The Irish War of Independence* (Dublin: Gill and Macmillan, 2002)

Alistair Horne, *A Savage War of Peace: Algeria 1954–1962* (New York: New York Review Books, 2006 [1977])

Matthew Hughes, *Britain's Pacification of Palestine: The British Army, the Colonial State, and the Arab Revolt, 1936–1939* (Cambridge: Cambridge University Press, 2019)

Denis Judd and Keith Surridge, *The Boer War: A History* (London: IB Tauris, 2013 [2002])

Mary Kaldor, *New Wars and Old Wars: Organized Violence in a Global Era* (Cambridge: Polity Press, 3rd ed. 2012, [1999])

Stanley Karnow, *Vietnam: A History* (London: Penguin, 1997 [1983])

George Kassimeris (ed.), *Warrior's Dishonour: Barbarity, Morality and Torture in Modern Warfare* (Abingdon, Routledge, 2016 [2006])

John Keegan, *A History of Warfare* (London: Random House, 1993)

Michael G. Kort, *The Vietnam War Reexamined* (Cambridge: Cambridge University Press, 2018)

Andrew F. Krepinevich, *The Army and Vietnam* (Baltimore, MD: Johns Hopkins University Press, 1986)

Frank Ledwidge, *Losing Small Wars: British Military Failure in the 9/11 Wars* (New Haven, CT: Yale University Press, 2017 [2011])

D. M. Leeson, *The Black and Tans: British Police and Auxiliaries in the Irish War of Independence* (Oxford: Oxford University Press, 2011)

Brian McAllister Linn, *The Philippine War 1899–1902* (Lawrence, KS, University Press of Kansas, 2000)

Shiraz Maher, *Salafi-Jihadism: The History of an Idea* (Oxford: Oxford University Press, 2016)

Peter R. Mansoor, *Surge: My Journey with General David Petraeus and the Remaking of the Iraq War* (New Haven: Yale University Press, 2014)

Daniel Marston and Carter Malkasian (eds), *Counterinsurgency in Modern Warfare* (Oxford: Osprey Publishing, 2010)

Mike Martin, *An Intimate War: An Oral History of the Helmand Conflict* (London: Hurst, 2014)

David McKittrick and David McVea, *Making Sense of the Troubles: A History of the Northern Ireland Conflict* (London: Viking, 2000)

Stuart Creighton Miller, *'Benevolent Assimilation': The American Conquest of the Philippines, 1899-1903* (New Haven, CT: Yale University Press, 1982)

Thomas Mockaitis, *British Counterinsurgency, 1919–60* (London: Macmillan, 1990)

Thomas Mockaitis, *British Counterinsurgency in the Post-Imperial Era* (Manchester: Manchester University Press, 1995)

Mark Moyar, *Triumph Forsaken: The Vietnam War, 1954–1965* (Cambridge: Cambridge University Press, 2006)

Andrew Mumford, *The Counterinsurgency Myth: The British Experience of Irregular Warfare* (Abingdon: Routledge, 2012)

John Nagl, *Learning to Eat Soup with a Knife: Counterinsurgency Lessons from Malaya and Vietnam* (Chicago: University of Chicago Press, 2005 [2002])

Peter R. Neumann, *Britain's Long War: British Strategy in the Northern Ireland Conflict, 1969–98* (Basingstoke: Palgrave Macmillan, 2003)

John Newsinger, *British Counter-Insurgency: From Palestine to Northern Ireland* (Basingstoke: Palgrave, 2002)

Victoria Nolan, *Military Leadership and Counterinsurgency: The British Army and Small War Strategy Since World War II* (London: I.B. Tauris, 2012)

Peter Paret, *French Revolutionary Warfare from Indochina to Algeria: The Analysis of a Political and Military Doctrine* (London: Pall Mall Press, 1964)

Peter Paret (ed.), *Makers of Modern Strategy: from Machiavelli to the Nuclear Age* (Oxford: Clarendon Press, 1986)

Jeffrey Record, *The Wrong War: Why We Lost in Vietnam* (Annapolis, MD: Naval Institute Press, 1998)

Paul Rich and Isabelle Duyvesteyn (eds), *The Routledge Handbook of Insurgency and Counterinsurgency* (Abingdon: Routledge, 2012)

Tim Ripley, *Operation Telic: The British Campaign in Iraq 2003–2009* (Telic-Herrick Publications, 2016)

William Sheehan, *A Hard Local War: The British Army and the Guerrilla War in Cork, 1919-1921* (Dublin: History Press Ireland, 2017 [2011])

Lewis Sorley, *A Better War: The Unexamined Victories and Final Tragedy of America's Last Years in Vietnam* (New York: Houghton Mifflin Harcourt, 1999)

Lewis Sorley, *Westmoreland: the General who Lost Vietnam* (New York: Houghton Mifflin Harcourt, 2011)

S. B. Spies, *Methods of Barbarism: Roberts and Kitchener and Civilians in the Boer Republics, January 1900–May 1902* (Jeppestown: Jonathan Ball, 2001)

Hew Strachan (ed.), *Big Wars and Small Wars: the British Army and the Lessons of War in the Twentieth Century* (Abingdon: Routledge, 2006)

Hew Strachan, *The Direction of War* (Cambridge: Cambridge University Press, 2013)

Harry G. Summers Jr., *On Strategy: A Critical Analysis of the Vietnam War* (New York City, NY, Presidio Press, 2nd ed. 1995, [1982])

Daniel E. Sutherland, *A Savage Conflict: The Decisive Role of Guerrillas in the American Civil War* (Chapel Hill: University of North Carolina Press, 2009)

Robert Taber, *War of the Flea* (Dulles: Brassey's, 2002 [1965])

Martin Thomas (ed.), *The French Colonial Mind, Volume 2: Violence, Military Encounters, and Colonialism* (Lincoln: University of Nebraska Press, 2011)

Martin Thomas, Fight or Flight: *Britain, France, and their Roads from Empire* (Oxford: Oxford University Press, 2014)

Charles Townshend, *The Republic: The Fight for Irish Independence* (London: Penguin, 2014 [2013])

André Wessels (ed.), *Lord Kitchener and the War in South Africa, 1899–1902* (Stroud: Sutton Publishing, 2006)

Articles

Martin Alexander and J. F. V. Keiger, 'France and the Algerian War: Strategy, Operations and Diplomacy', *Journal of Strategic Studies*, 25: 2 (2002)

Dale Andrade, 'Westmoreland was Right: Learning the Wrong Lessons from the Vietnam War', *Small Wars and Insurgencies*, 19: 2 (2008)

Ian Beckett, 'Robert Thompson and the British advisory mission to South Vietnam, 1961–1965', *Small Wars & Insurgencies*, 8: 3 (1997)

Andrew J. Birtle, 'PROVN, Westmoreland, and the Historians: A Reappraisal', *Journal of Military History*, 72: 4 (2008)

Tom Bowden, 'The Politics of the Arab Rebellion in Palestine 1936–39', *Middle Eastern Studies*, 11: 2 (1975)

Daniel Branch, 'Footprints in the Sand: British Colonial Counterinsurgency and the War in Iraq', *Politics and Society*, 38: 1 (2010)

Peter Busch, 'Supporting the War: Britain's Decision to send the Thompson Mission to Vietnam, 1960–61', *Cold War History*, 2: 1 (2001)

Peter Busch, 'Killing the "Vietcong": The British Advisory Mission and the Strategic Hamlet Programme', *Journal of Strategic Studies*, 25: 1 (2002)

David Charters, 'Counter-Insurgency Intelligence: The Evolution of British Theory and Practice', *Journal of Conflict Studies*, 29 (2009)

Paul Cheeseright, 'Involvement Without Engagement: the British Advisory Mission in South Vietnam, 16 September 1961–31 March 1965', *Asian Affairs*, 42: 2 (2011)

Loo Chow Chin, 'The Repatriation of the Chinese as a Counter-Insurgency Policy During the Malayan Emergency', *Journal of Southeast Asian Studies*, 45: 3 (2014)

Christopher Cradock and M. L. R. Smith, '"No Fixed Values": A Reinterpretation of the Influence of the Theory of *Guerre Révolutionnaire* and the Battle of Algiers, 1956–1957', *Journal of Cold War Studies*, 9: 4 (2007)

Gregory A. Daddis, 'The Problem of Metrics: Assessing Progress and Effectiveness in the Vietnam War', *War in History*, 19: 1 (2012)

Gregory A. Daddis, 'Eating Soup with a Spoon: The US Army as a "Learning Organization" in the Vietnam War', *Journal of Military History*, 77: 1 (2013)

Brice Dickson, 'Counter-Insurgency and Human Rights in Northern Ireland', *Journal of Strategic Studies*, 32: 3 (2009)

Paul Dixon, '"Hearts and Minds"? British Counter-Insurgency from Malaya to Iraq', *Journal of Strategic Studies*, 32: 3 (2009)

Michael Finch, 'Total War of the Mind: The French Theory of la guerre révolutionnaire, 1954–1958', *War in History*, 25: 3 (2018)

Gian Gentile, '"A Strategy of Tactics: Population-Centric COIN and the Army', *Parameters*, 34 (2009)

Gian Gentile, 'The Selective Use of History in the Development of American Counterinsurgency Doctrine', *Army History*, 72 (2009)

Colin S. Gray, 'Irregular Warfare: One Nature, Many Characters', *Strategic Studies Quarterly*, 1: 2 (2007)

Jonathan Gumz, 'Reframing the Historical Problematic of Insurgency: How the Professional Military Literature Created a New History and Missed the Past', *Journal of Strategic Studies*, 32: 4 (2009)

Karl Hack, 'The Malayan Emergency as Counter-Insurgency Paradigm', *Journal of Strategic Studies*, 32: 3 (2009)

Karl Hack, 'Everyone Lived in Fear: Malaya and the British Way of Counter-Insurgency', *Small Wars and Insurgencies*, 23: 4-5 (2012)

Matthew Hughes, 'The Banality of Brutality: British Armed Forces and the Repression of the Arab Revolt in Palestine, 1936–1939', *English Historical Review*, 124: 507 (2009)

Matthew Hughes, 'From Law and Order to Pacification: Britain's Suppression of the Arab Revolt in Palestine, 1936–39', *Journal of Palestine Studies*, 39: 2 (2010)

Matthew Hughes, 'Terror in Galilee: British-Jewish Collaboration and the Special Night Squads in Palestine during the Arab Revolt, 1938–39', *Journal of Imperial and Commonwealth history*, 43: 4 (2015)

Preston Jordan Lim, 'The Prickly Thorn: A Re-evaluation of Orde Wingate and the Special Night Squads', *Small wars & insurgencies*, 29:1 (2018)

John Lonsdale, 'Constructing Mau Mau', *Transactions of the Royal Historical Society*, 40 (1990)

Martin J. McCleery, 'Debunking the Myths of Operation Demetrius: The Introduction of Internment in Northern Ireland in 1971', *Irish Political Studies*, 27: 3 (2012)

Jacob Norris, 'Repression and Rebellion: Britain's Response to the Arab Revolt in Palestine of 1936-39', *Journal of Imperial and Commonwealth History*, 36: 1 (2008)

Andrew R. Novo, 'Friend or Foe? The Cyprus Police Force and the EOKA Insurgency', *Small Wars and Insurgencies*, 23: 3 (2012)

Bernard Porter, 'How Did They Get Away with It?', *London Review of Books*, 27: 5 (2005)

Kumar Ramakrishna, 'Anatomy of a Collapse: Explaining the Malayan Communist Mass Surrenders of 1958', *War and Society*, 21: 2 (2003)

Kumar Ramakrishna, '"Bribing the Reds to Give Up": Rewards Policy in the Malayan Emergency', *War in History*, 9: 3 (2009)

Anthony Short, 'The Malayan Emergency and the Batang Kali Incident', *Asian Affairs*, 41: 3 (2010)

Andrew Silke, 'Ferocious Times: The IRA, the RIC, and Britain's Failure in 1919–1921', *Terrorism and Political Violence*, 28: 3 (2016)

Iain R. Smith and Andreas Stucki, 'The Colonial Development of Concentration Camps', *Journal of Imperial and Commonwealth History*, 39: 3 (2011)

M. L. R. Smith and Peter R. Neumann, 'Motorman's Long Journey: Changing the Strategic Setting in Northern Ireland', *Contemporary British History*, 19: 4 (2005)

Hew Strachan, 'British Counter-Insurgency from Malaya to Iraq', *RUSI Journal*, 152: 6 (2007)

Martin Thomas, 'The British Government and the End of French Algeria, 1958–62', *Journal of Strategic Studies*, 25: 2 (2002)

Marie-Cecile Thoral, 'French Colonial Counter-Insurgency: General Bugeaud and the Conquest of Algeria, 1840–47', *British Journal of Military History*, 1: 2 (2015)

Rod Thornton, 'Getting It Wrong: The Crucial Mistakes Made in the Early Stages of the British Army's Deployment to Northern Ireland (August 1969 to March 1972', *Journal of Strategic Studies*, 30: 1 (2007)

Charles Townshend, 'The Irish Republican Army and the Development of Guerrilla Warfare, 1916–1921', *English Historical Review*, 94: 371 (1979)

Charles Townshend, 'The Defence of Palestine: Insurrection and Public Security, 1936-1939', *English Historical Review*, 103: 409 (1988)

Irvin M. Wall, 'De Gaulle, the "Anglo-Saxons", and the Algerian War', *Journal of Strategic Studies*, 25: 2 (2002)

André Wessels, 'Boer Guerrilla and British Counter-Guerrilla Operations in South Africa, 1899 to 1902', *Scientia Militaria, South African Journal of Military Studies*, 39: 2 (2011)

Index

Abrams, General Creighton, 56
Aden Emergency, xvii
Aguinaldo, Emilio, 16–17
Air policing, 149
Al-Assad, Bashar, xix
Algeria, xxvii, 7, 36–45, 59, 73,
    149–150
Al-Qaeda, 98–100, 108, 110, 112, 114
American Civil War, 2
American War of Independence, 2
Amritsar massacre, 29
Angolan War of Independence, xxvii,
    59
Arab Revolt, xvi, 19, 26, 31

Ba'athist regime, xix, 97, 98, 105, 112
Bamiyan, 100
Bao Dai, 49–50
Baring, Sir Evelyn, 73, 79
bin Laden, Osama, 98–100, 143
Blockhouses, 13
Bremer, Paul 'Jerry', 97–98, 110,
    114–115
Briggs Plan, 67
Bugeaud, Marshal Thomas-Robert,
    7–9
Bush, President George W., xi–xiii,
    97–99, 102–104, 107, 120, 123,
    128–129

Central Office for South Vietnam
    (COSVN), 56
Challe Plan, 43
Chilcot Report, 103–104, 108, 110,
    116, 119, 121, 124, 127, 129
Chin Peng, xxiii, 65, 67, 69, 71
Callwell, Charles E., 5–11, 30, 32, 148
Cinquième Bureau, 42
Civil Operations and Rural
    Development Support (CORDS),
    54–55
Clausewitz, Carl von, xviii–xx, xxii
Coalition Provisional Authority
    (CPA), 97–98, 109–111, 114–116,
    118, 121
Collins, Michael, 21–22, 24, 26
colonisation, xxiv, 44, 59 63–64, 78,
    143, 149
concentration camps, 30 33–34 36 87
    146
conventional war, xi–xvii, xxii–xxiii,
    5, 11–12, 33, 37, 45–49, 52–58,
    86–87, 119, 151
counterinsurgency
    'British approach', 14 16 73 101
        xvii, xx, 61, 95
    definition of, xiii–xxv
    theories of, xiii, xxv, 44–47, 54,
        83–87, 95, 147, 149

French approach, 2, 7–8, 35–45, 59
US approach, xi–xii, 2, 47–59,
  97–134, 140–144

Diem, Ngo Dinh, 49–51, 86

Erskine, General Sir George, 73–76
Ethniki Organosis Kypriou Agoniston
  (EOKA) (National Organization of
  Cypriot Struggle), 79–83

Filipino Army of Liberation, 16–17
Francs-tireurs, 4
Free Syrian Army, xix, xxvii
French Revolutionary War, 2, 37

Galliéni, Joseph, 7–8, 36
Galula, David, 35, 44–47, 87, 95, 144,
  147, 149–151
Gaulle, Charles de, 42–43
Gentile, Gian, xvi, 95
guerre révolutionnaire, 35–37, 41, 45,
  149
Gurney, Sir Henry, 66–68

Harding, Field Marshal Sir John, 74,
  81–82
Ho Chi Minh, 47
Hussein, Saddam, 98, 102

Ia Drang Valley, 55
improvised explosive devices (IEDs),
  122, 139–141
insurgency
  definition of, xiv–xxii
  Maoist, xxi, xxii, 36, 54
International Security Assistance
  Force (ISAF), 101, 134, 137–142,
  144

Iraq, xi–xxii, 19, 58, 62–63, 95, 97–98,
  101–134, 142–144, 150–151
Ireland, xxv, 19–22, 25–26, 30–31,
  63–64, 86–95, 150
Irish War of Independence, xxvii,
  20–26

Johnson, President Lyndon B., 51,
  54, 56

Kenya, xxvii, 63–65, 71–81, 83,
  86–87, 89, 94–95, 149–150
Kitson, General Sir Frank, 64–65,
  86–88, 143, 148, 151
Kikuyu people, 73–74, 77

La Guerrilla, 2
Lieber Code (General Orders No.
  100), 3
Lawrence, T. E., xvi, 19
Lyautey, Hubert, 7–8, 32, 36, 38

McLean Court of Inquiry, 75–77
McLean, Lieutenant-General Sir
  Kenneth, 75–77
Macready, General Sir Nevil, 25
Malaya, xxiii–xxv, 52, 61–71, 77,
  79–86, 89, 94–95, 149–150
Malayan Communist Party (MCP),
  xxiii, 65–67, 69–71, 85
Malayan National Liberation Army
  (MNLA), 66–67
Mao Zedong, 32
Massu, General Jacques, 41, 43–44
Mau Mau, 63, 72–80, 86–87
Military Assistance Command,
  Vietnam (MACV), 51, 56
Min Yuen (Masses Organisation)
  xxiii, 66–67

Mozambique Liberation Front (*Frente de Libertação de Moçambique*, FRELIMO), 59
Musa Qala, 135–137, 139

National Liberation Front (*Front de Libération Nationale* or FLN), xvii, 37–44, 50
'new-model drives', 15
'New Villages', 67, 85
Northern Alliance, 99–100
Northern Ireland, xxv, xxvii, 63–64, 86–95, 150

'oil spot' method, 9, 54, 135
Omar, Mullah, 49, 98–101
Operation *Anvil*, 73, 75
Operation *Banner*, 63, 87, 93–94
Operation *Charge of the Knights*, 131–132
Operation *Demetrius*, 90
Operation *Forward to Victory*, 81
Operations *Herrick IV–VI*, 138–140
Operation *Iraqi Freedom*, xii, xxviii
Operation *Jock Scott*, 73
Operation *Jumelles* (Binoculars), 43
Operation *Masher/White Wing*, 55
Operation *Motorman*, 91–92
Operation *Rolling Thunder*, 55
Operation *Salamanca*, 125
Operation *Sinbad*, 126–128, 130, 132
Operation *Sond Chara*, 139
Operation *Steel Curtain*, 120
Operations *Thayer, Irving*, and *Thayer II, Cedar Falls*, 56
Operation *Together Forward/Together Forward II*, 124
Organisation Armée Secrète (OAS), 43–44

Pakistan, 101, 143
Peninsular War (1807–14), 2
Petraeus, Major-General David, 113, 118, 131, 133, 141
Petraeus Plan, 118
Powell, Colin, xix, 102
psychological warfare, 14, 42

Revolutionary Armed Forces of Colombia (FARC), xx
Rey, Koos de la, 12
Royal Irish Constabulary (RIC), 21–23

Sands, Bobby, 93
Scorched-earth tactics, 13
Sections Administratives Spécialisées (SAS), 42
Sections Administratives Urbaines (SAU), 42
Sinn Féin, 21, 26, 93–94
small war, 1–4, 8, 30–31, 148
Smith, Brigadier-General Jacob H., 17–18
South African War, xxvii, 5, 9–10, 25, 27, 64, 66, 77, 149
Special Air Service (SAS), xvii, 93, 106
Special Night Squads (SNS), 28
Straw, Jack, 104, 109, 123
Suez Crisis, 40–41, 82
Summers, Colonel Harry, xx, 48–49

Tehrik-i-Taliban Pakistan (TTP), xxi
Templer, General Sir Gerald, 68–71, 74
Terrorism, xiii–xvi, xxii–xxiii, 99
Trinquier, Roger, 35, 44–45, 47, 87, 95, 151

Türk Mukavemet Teşkilatı (Turkish Resistance Organisation/TMT), 82

United Nations, 39, 80

Vietnam War (1954–75), xxvii, 36–37, 47–48, 51, 53, 59, 149–150

Viet Minh, 35–37, 54

Waller, Major Littleton W. T., 18

weapons of mass destruction (WMD), 102–103, 105

Westmoreland, General William C., 51, 53–57, 86, 149

Wet, Christiaan de, 12, 15

Weyler, Captain-General Valeriano, 12, 17

'wondrous trinity', xix